OLD Mr.

De Luxe

Boston

Official

Bartender's

Guide

A Collection of Recipes
for Mixed Drinks to Suit
Every Taste and Occasion

Compiled and Edited by Leo Cotton

PUBLISHED BY
MR. BOSTON DISTILLER INC. BOSTON, MASSACHUSETTS

1st printing January 1935
2nd printing March 1935
3rd printing October 1936
4th printing (revised) September 1940
5th printing October 1941
6th printing November 1946
7th printing December 1948
8th printing September 1949
9th printing February 1951
10th printing April 1953
11th printing December 1953
12th printing (revised) July 1955
13th printing September 1957
14th printing May 1959
15th printing December 1959
16th printing (revised) August 1960
17th printing January 1961
18th printing June 1961
19th printing September 1961
20th printing October 1961
21st printing December 1962
22nd printing January 1963

LIBRARY OF CONGRESS CATALOG NUMBER: 60–15939

Acknowledgements

THE DEEPEST APPRECIATION is acknowledged to Alfred Bourassa for his valuable contribution which has helped make this book one of the most complete of its kind; and to Joseph DeSoto, founder and chief instructor of the original Boston Bartender's School and to the many other bartenders who contributed their assistance.

EDITOR

Contents

An Introduction to
the Art of Good
Mixing and Good Living

THE FIRST edition of the OLD MR. BOSTON OFFICIAL BAR-
TENDER'S GUIDE was published in 1935 to provide an authentic
and accurate recipe book. It was dedicated to the thousands of
bartenders throughout the country and to all others who felt
the need for an official source of information for mixing drinks.

Since that date more than two million copies have been sold
and to commemorate the Silver Anniversary edition issued in
1960, it was completely revised from cover to cover. Handsome
new color pages were included with an easier to read format. Special sections on Eggnogs, The Martini, Bar Hints and Measure-
ments were added together with a Liquor Dictionary and many
new recipes. The demand has been so great that this reprint is
now necessary and as it is the desire of the editor to constantly
keep this book up to date, additional revisions and drinks which
have become popular, even in the short time since the last edition, are now included. It is gratifying to learn from the innumer-
able letters which have been received that this book is considered
one of the finest and most authentic drink-recipe books ever published.

Old Mr. Boston will appear frequently throughout the pages
of this book. He is a rare and versatile gentleman, everlastingly
young and ever ready to accept the difficult role of host. Follow the advice of this joyful and genial friend and there will be
many pleasant times in store for you. We know you are going
to like Old Mr. Boston.

A

ABBEY COCKTAIL

1½ oz. Old Mr. Boston Dry Gin
Juice of ¼ Orange
1 Dash Orange Bitters
*Shake well with cracked ice and
strain into 3 oz. cocktail glass. Add
a Maraschino cherry.*

ABSINTHE COCKTAIL

1½ oz. Absinthe Substitute
¾ oz. Water
¼ oz. Old Mr. Boston Anisette
1 Dash Orange Bitters
*Shake well with cracked ice and
strain into 3 oz. cocktail glass.*

ABSINTHE DRIP COCKTAIL

*Pour 1½ oz. absinthe substitute into
special drip glass or Old Fashioned
cocktail glass. Place cube of sugar
over hole of drip spoon (or in silver
tea strainer). Pack spoon or strainer
with cracked ice, pour cold water to
fill. When water has dripped through,
drink is ready.*

ABSINTHE SPECIAL COCKTAIL

1½ oz. Absinthe Substitute
1 oz. Water
¼ Teaspoon Powdered Sugar
1 Dash Orange Bitters
*Shake well with cracked ice and
strain into 3 oz. cocktail glass.*

ADONIS COCKTAIL

1 Dash Orange Bitters
¾ oz. Sweet Vermouth
1½ oz. Dry Sherry Wine
*Stir well with cracked ice and strain
into 3 oz. cocktail glass.*

AFFINITY COCKTAIL

¾ oz. Dry Vermouth
¾ oz. Sweet Vermouth
¾ oz. Old Mr. Boston Scotch
  Whisky
2 Dashes Orange Bitters
*Stir well with cracked ice and strain
into 3 oz. cocktail glass.*

AFTER DINNER COCKTAIL

1 oz. Old Mr. Boston Apricot
  Flavored Brandy
1 oz. Curacao
Juice of 1 lime
*Shake well with cracked ice and
strain into 3 oz. cocktail glass. Leave
lime in glass.*

A

AFTER SUPPER COCKTAIL

1 oz. Old Mr. Boston Apricot
    Flavored Brandy
1 oz. Curacao
½ Teaspoon Lemon Juice
*Shake well with cracked ice and
strain into 3 oz. cocktail glass.*

ALABAMA COCKTAIL

½ oz. Lemon Juice
½ Teaspoon Powdered Sugar
1½ oz. Old Mr. Boston Five Star
    Brandy
1 Teaspoon Curacao
*Shake well with cracked ice and
strain into 3 oz. cocktail glass.*

ALABAMA FIZZ

Juice ½ Lemon
1 Teaspoon Powdered Sugar
2 oz. Old Mr. Boston Dry Gin
*Shake well with cracked ice and
strain into 7 oz. highball glass. Fill
with carbonated water. Add 2 sprigs
of fresh mint.*

ALASKA COCKTAIL

2 Dashes Orange Bitters
1½ oz. Old Mr. Boston Dry Gin
¾ oz. Yellow Chartreuse
*Stir well with cracked ice and strain
into 3 oz. cocktail glass.*

ALBEMARLE FIZZ

Juice ½ Lemon
1 Teaspoon Powdered Sugar
2 oz. Old Mr. Boston Dry Gin
*Shake well with cracked ice and
strain into 7 oz. highball glass. Fill
with carbonated water. Add 1 teaspoon raspberry syrup.*

ALEXANDER COCKTAIL No. 1

1 oz. Old Mr. Boston Dry Gin
1 oz. Old Mr. Boston Creme de
    Cacao
1 oz. Sweet Cream
*Shake well with cracked ice and
strain into 4 oz. cocktail glass.*

ALEXANDER COCKTAIL No. 2

1 oz. Old Mr. Boston Creme de
    Cacao
1 oz. Old Mr. Boston Five Star
    Brandy
1 oz. Sweet Cream
*Shake well with cracked ice and
strain into 4 oz. cocktail glass.*

ALEXANDER'S SISTER COCKTAIL

1 oz. Old Mr. Boston Dry Gin
1 oz. Old Mr. Boston Creme de
    Menthe (green)
1 oz. Sweet Cream
*Shake well with cracked ice and
strain into 4 oz. cocktail glass.*

ALLEN COCKTAIL

¼ oz. Lemon Juice
¾ oz. Maraschino
1½ oz. Old Mr. Boston Dry Gin
*Shake well with cracked ice and
strain into 3 oz. cocktail glass.*

ALLIES COCKTAIL

1 oz. Dry Vermouth
1 oz. Old Mr. Boston Dry Gin
½ Teaspoon Old Mr. Boston
    Kummel
*Stir well with cracked ice and strain
into 3 oz. cocktail glass.*

A

AMER PICON COCKTAIL

Juice 1 Lime
1 Teaspoon Grenadine
½ oz. Amer Picon
Shake well with cracked ice and strain into 3 oz. cocktail glass.

AMERICAN BEAUTY COCKTAIL

1 oz. Orange Juice
1 oz. Grenadine
1 oz. Dry Vermouth
1 oz. Old Mr. Boston Five Star Brandy
1 Teaspoon Old Mr. Boston Creme de Menthe (white)
Shake well with cracked ice and strain into 3 oz. cocktail glass and top with a little Port Wine.

AMERICAN GROG

1 Lump of Sugar
Juice ¼ Lemon
1½ oz. Old Mr. Boston Imported Rum
Fill hot whiskey glass with hot water and stir.

ANGEL'S DELIGHT

1 oz. Grenadine
1 oz. Triple Sec
1 oz. Creme de Yvette
1 oz. Fresh Cream
Pour carefully, in order given, into Pousse Café glass, so that each ingredient floats on preceding one.

ANGEL'S KISS

¼ oz. Old Mr. Boston Creme de Cacao
¼ oz. Creme de Yvette
¼ oz. Old Mr. Boston Five Star Brandy
¼ oz. Sweet Cream
Pour ingredients carefully, in order given, so that they do not mix. Use Pousse Café glass.

ANGEL'S TIP

¾ oz. Old Mr. Boston Creme de Cacao
¼ oz. Sweet Cream
Float cream and insert toothpick in cherry and put on top. Use Pousse Café glass.

ANGEL'S WING

⅓ oz. Old Mr. Boston Creme de Cacao
⅓ oz. Old Mr. Boston Five Star Brandy
⅓ oz. Sweet Cream
Pour ingredients carefully, in order given, so that they do not mix. Use Pousse Café glass.

APPLE BLOW FIZZ

White of 1 Egg
Juice ½ Lemon
1 Teaspoon Powdered Sugar
2 oz. Apple Brandy
Shake well with cracked ice and strain into 8 oz. highball glass. Fill with carbonated water.

3

APPLE BRANDY COCKTAIL

1½ oz. Apple Brandy
1 Teaspoon Grenadine
1 Teaspoon Lemon Juice
Shake well with cracked ice and strain into 3 oz. cocktail glass.

APPLE BRANDY HIGHBALL

1 Cube of Ice
2 oz. Apple Brandy
Fill 8 oz. highball glass with ginger ale or carbonated water. Add twist of lemon peel, if desired, and stir.

APPLE BRANDY RICKEY

1 Cube of Ice
Juice of ½ Lime
1½ oz. Apple Brandy
Fill 8 oz. highball glass with carbonated water and stir. Leave lime in glass.

APPLE BRANDY SOUR

Juice ½ Lemon
½ Teaspoon Powdered Sugar
2 oz. Apple Brandy
Shake well with cracked ice and strain into 6 oz. sour glass. Fill with carbonated water and stir. Decorate with a slice of lemon and a cherry.

APPLE PIE COCKTAIL

¾ oz. Old Mr. Boston Imported Rum
¾ oz. Sweet Vermouth
1 Teaspoon Old Mr. Boston Apricot Flavored Brandy
½ Teaspoon Grenadine
1 Teaspoon Lemon Juice
Shake well with cracked ice and strain into 3 oz. cocktail glass.

APRICOT BRANDY RICKEY

1 Cube of Ice
Juice of ½ Lime
2 oz. Old Mr. Boston Apricot Flavored Brandy
Fill 8 oz. highball glass with carbonated water and stir. Leave lime in glass.

APRICOT COCKTAIL

Juice of ¼ Lemon
Juice of ¼ Orange
1½ oz. Old Mr. Boston Apricot Flavored Brandy
1 Teaspoon Old Mr. Boston Dry Gin
Shake well with cracked ice and strain into 3 oz. cocktail glass.

APRICOT COOLER

Into 12 oz. Tom Collins glass, put
½ Teaspoon Powdered Sugar
2 oz. Carbonated Water
Stir and fill glass with cracked ice and add:
2 oz. Old Mr. Boston Apricot Flavored Brandy
Fill with carbonated water or ginger ale and stir again. Insert spiral of orange or lemon peel (or both) and dangle end over rim of glass.

APRICOT FIZZ

Juice ½ Lemon
Juice ½ Lime
1 Teaspoon Powdered Sugar
2 oz. Old Mr. Boston Apricot Flavored Brandy
Shake well with cracked ice and strain into 7 oz. highball glass. Fill with carbonated water.

B & B

½ oz. Benedictine
½ oz. Cognac
*Use cordial glass and carefully float
the Cognac on top of the Benedictine.*

Babbie's Special Cocktail

2 oz. Sweet Cream
½ oz. Old Mr. Boston Apricot
Flavored Brandy
¼ Teaspoon Old Mr. Boston Dry
Gin
*Shake well with cracked ice and
strain into 3 oz. cocktail glass.*

Bacardi Cocktail

½ oz. Bacardi Rum
Juice ½ Lime
2 Teaspoon Grenadine
*Shake well with cracked ice and
strain into 3 oz. cocktail glass.*

Bachelor's Bait Cocktail

½ oz. Old Mr. Boston Dry Gin
White of 1 Egg
Dash Orange Bitters
2 Teaspoon Grenadine
*Shake well with cracked ice and
strain into 4 oz. cocktail glass.*

Baltimore Bracer Cocktail

1 oz. Old Mr. Boston Anisette
1 oz. Old Mr. Boston Five Star
Brandy
White of 1 Egg
*Shake well with cracked ice and
strain into 4 oz. cocktail glass.*

Baltimore Eggnog

1 Egg
1 Teaspoon Powdered Sugar
1 oz. Old Mr. Boston Five Star
Brandy
1 oz. Jamaica Rum
1 oz. Madeira Wine
*Fill glass with milk, shake well with
cracked ice and strain into 12 oz.
Tom Collins glass. Grate nutmeg on
top.*

Bamboo Cocktail

1½ oz. Sherry Wine
¾ oz. Dry Vermouth
1 Dash Orange Bitters
*Stir well with cracked ice and strain
into 3 oz. cocktail glass.*

BANANA PUNCH

2 oz. Old Mr. Boston Vodka
¾ oz. Old Mr. Boston Apricot
    Flavored Brandy
Juice ½ Lime
*Pour into 12 oz. Tom Collins glass
filled with crushed ice. Add carbonated water and top with sprigs of
mint.*

BARBARY COAST COCKTAIL

½ oz. Old Mr. Boston Dry Gin
½ oz. Old Mr. Boston Imported
    Rum
½ oz. Old Mr. Boston Creme de
    Cacao
½ oz. Old Mr. Boston Scotch
    Whisky
½ oz. Sweet Cream
*Shake well with cracked ice and
strain into 4 oz. cocktail glass.*

BARON COCKTAIL

½ oz. Dry Vermouth
1½ oz. Old Mr. Boston Dry Gin
1½ Teaspoons Curacao
½ Teaspoon Sweet Vermouth
*Stir well with cracked ice and strain
into 3 oz. cocktail glass. Add twist of
lemon peel and drop in glass.*

BARTON SPECIAL COCKTAIL

½ oz. Apple Brandy
½ oz. Old Mr. Boston Scotch
    Whisky
½ oz. Old Mr. Boston Dry Gin
*Stir well with cracked ice and strain
into 3 oz. cocktail glass.*

BEADLESTONE COCKTAIL

1¼ oz. Dry Vermouth
1¼ oz. Old Mr. Boston Scotch
    Whisky
*Stir well with cracked ice and strain
into 3 oz. cocktail glass.*

BEALS COCKTAIL

1½ oz. Old Mr. Boston Scotch
    Whisky
½ oz. Dry Vermouth
½ oz. Sweet Vermouth
*Stir well with cracked ice and strain
into 3 oz. cocktail glass.*

BEAUTY SPOT COCKTAIL

1 Teaspoon Orange Juice
½ oz. Sweet Vermouth
½ oz. Dry Vermouth
1 oz. Old Mr. Boston Dry Gin
*Shake well with cracked ice and
strain into 3 oz. cocktail glass, with
a dash of grenadine in bottom of
glass.*

BELMONT COCKTAIL

2 oz. Old Mr. Boston Dry Gin
1 Teaspoon Raspberry Syrup
¾ oz. Sweet Cream
*Shake well with cracked ice and
strain into 4 oz. cocktail glass.*

BENNETT COCKTAIL

Juice of ½ Lime
1½ oz. Old Mr. Boston Dry Gin
½ Teaspoon Powdered Sugar
2 Dashes Orange Bitters
*Shake well with cracked ice and
strain into 3 oz. cocktail glass.*

BERMUDA BOUQUET

Juice ¼ Orange
Juice ½ Lemon
1 Teaspoon Powdered Sugar
1½ oz. Old Mr. Boston Dry Gin
1 oz. Old Mr. Boston Apricot
    Flavored Brandy
1 Teaspoon Grenadine
½ Teaspoon Curacao
*Shake well with cracked ice and
strain into 8 oz. highball glass.*

BERMUDA HIGHBALL

1 Cube of Ice
¾ oz. Old Mr. Boston Dry Gin
¾ oz. Old Mr. Boston Five Star
    Brandy
¾ oz. Dry Vermouth
*Fill 8 oz. highball glass with ginger
ale or carbonated water. Add twist
of lemon peel, if desired, and stir.*

BERMUDA ROSE COCKTAIL

1¼ oz. Old Mr. Boston Dry Gin
¼ oz. Old Mr. Boston Apricot
    Flavored Brandy
¼ oz. Grenadine
*Shake well with cracked ice and
strain into 3 oz. cocktail glass.*

BETWEEN THE SHEETS
COCKTAIL

Juice ¼ Lemon
½ oz. Old Mr. Boston Five Star
    Brandy
½ oz. Triple Sec
½ oz. Old Mr. Boston Imported
    Rum
*Shake well with cracked ice and
strain into 3 oz. cocktail glass.*

BIFFY COCKTAIL

Juice of ½ Lemon
½ oz. Swedish Punch
1½ oz. Old Mr. Boston Dry Gin
*Shake well with cracked ice and
strain into 3 oz. cocktail glass.*

BIJOU COCKTAIL

¾ oz. Old Mr. Boston Dry Gin
¾ oz. Green Chartreuse
¾ oz. Sweet Vermouth
1 Dash Orange Bitters
*Stir well with cracked ice and strain
into 3 oz. cocktail glass. Add cherry
on top.*

BILLY TAYLOR

Juice ½ Lime
2 Cubes of Ice
2 oz. Old Mr. Boston Dry Gin
*Fill 12 oz. Tom Collins glass with
carbonated water and stir gently.*

BIRD OF PARADISE FIZZ

Juice ½ Lemon
1 Teaspoon Powdered Sugar
White of 1 Egg
1 Teaspoon Grenadine
2 oz. Old Mr. Boston Dry Gin
*Shake well with cracked ice and
strain into 8 oz. highball glass. Fill
with carbonated water.*

BISHOP

Juice ¼ Lemon
Juice ¼ Orange
1 Teaspoon Powdered Sugar
*Shake well with cracked ice and
strain into 8 oz. highball glass. Add
cube of ice, fill with Burgundy and
stir well. Decorate with fruits.*

Bitters Highball

1 Cube of Ice
¼ oz. Bitters
Fill 8 oz. highball glass with ginger ale or carbonated water. Add twist of lemon peel, if desired, and stir.

Black Hawk Cocktail

¼ oz. Old Mr. Boston Whiskey*
¼ oz. Old Mr. Boston Sloe Gin
Stir well with cracked ice and strain into 3 oz. cocktail glass. Serve with a cherry.

Black Magic

½ oz. Old Mr. Boston Vodka
1 oz. Expresso Coffee Liqueur
Dash of Lemon Juice.
Stir and serve in Old Fashioned cocktail glass with cubes of ice and twist of lemon peel.

Black Russian

Pour:
½ oz. Old Mr. Boston Vodka
1 oz. Kahlúa (Coffee Liqueur)
On ice cubes in Old Fashioned cocktail glass.

Black Velvet

1 oz. Stout
1 oz. Champagne
Pour very carefully into 12 oz. glass with cubes of ice and stir very gently.

Blarney Stone Cocktail

2 oz. Irish Whiskey
½ Teaspoon Absinthe Substitute
½ Teaspoon Curacao
¼ Teaspoon Maraschino
1 Dash Bitters
Shake well with cracked ice and strain into 3 oz. cocktail glass. Twist of orange peel and serve with an olive.

Blood and Sand Cocktail

½ oz. Orange Juice
½ oz. Old Mr. Boston Scotch Whisky
½ oz. Old Mr. Boston Wild Cherry Flavored Brandy
½ oz. Sweet Vermouth
Shake well with cracked ice and strain into 3 oz. cocktail glass.

Blood Bronx Cocktail

1½ oz. Old Mr. Boston Dry Gin
¼ oz. Dry Vermouth
Juice of ¼ Blood Orange
Shake well with cracked ice and strain into 3 oz. cocktail glass.

Bloodhound Cocktail

½ oz. Dry Vermouth
½ oz. Sweet Vermouth
1 oz. Old Mr. Boston Dry Gin
2 or 3 crushed Strawberries
Shake well with cracked ice and strain into 3 oz. cocktail glass.

*Bourbon, Blended, Rye or Canadian.

BLOODY BLOODY MARY COCKTAIL

1½ oz. Old Mr. Boston Vodka
3 oz. Tomato Juice
Juice ½ Lemon
Pinch Salt, Pepper and Celery Salt
½ Teaspoon Worcestershire Sauce
¼ Teaspoon Powdered Sugar
Shake well with cracked ice and strain into 6 oz. Old Fashioned cocktail glass with cube of ice. Decorate with sprig of fresh mint.

BLOODY MARY COCKTAIL

1½ oz. Old Mr. Boston Vodka
1½ oz. Tomato Juice
1 Dash Lemon Juice
Shake well with cracked ice and strain into Old Fashioned cocktail glass with cube of ice.

BLUE BLAZER

Use two large silver-plated mugs, with handles.
2½ oz. Old Mr. Boston Whiskey*
2½ oz. Boiling Water
Put the whiskey into one mug, and the boiling water into the other. Ignite the whiskey and, while blazing, mix both ingredients by pouring them four or five times from one mug to the other. If well done, this will have the appearance of a continued stream of liquid fire.
Sweeten with 1 teaspoon of Powdered Sugar and serve with a piece of lemon peel. Serve in 4 oz. hot whiskey glass.

BLUE DEVIL COCKTAIL

1 oz. Old Mr. Boston Dry Gin
Juice ½ Lemon or 1 Lime
½ oz. Maraschino
½ Teaspoon Creme de Yvette
Shake well with cracked ice an strain into 3 oz. cocktail glass.

BLUE MONDAY COCKTAIL

1½ oz. Old Mr. Boston Vodka
¾ oz. Triple Sec
1 Dash Blue Vegetable Coloring
Stir well with cracked ice and stra into 3 oz. cocktail glass.

BLUE MOON COCKTAIL

1½ oz. Old Mr. Boston Dry Gin
¾ oz. Creme de Yvette
Stir well with cracked ice and stra into 3 oz. cocktail glass. Add twist lemon peel and drop in glass.

BOBBY BURNS COCKTAIL

1¼ oz. Sweet Vermouth
1¼ oz. Old Mr. Boston Scotc
  Whisky
1 Teaspoon Benedictine
Stir well with cracked ice and stra into 3 oz. cocktail glass. Add twist lemon peel and drop in glass.

BOLERO COCKTAIL

1½ oz. Old Mr. Boston Import
  Rum
¾ oz. Apple Brandy
¼ Teaspoon Sweet Vermouth
Stir well with cracked ice and stre into 3 oz. cocktail glass.

* *Bourbon, Blended, Rye or Canadi*

Bronze Label Kentucky Straight Bourbon 86 Proof

BOLO COCKTAIL

2 oz. Old Mr. Boston Imported
    Rum
Juice of ½ Lime
Juice of ¼ Orange
1 Teaspoon Powdered Sugar
Shake well with cracked ice and
strain into 4 oz. cocktail glass.

BOMBAY COCKTAIL

½ oz. Dry Vermouth
½ oz. Sweet Vermouth
1 oz. Old Mr. Boston Five Star
    Brandy
¼ Teaspoon Absinthe Substitute
½ Teaspoon Curacao
Stir well with cracked ice and strain
into 3 oz. cocktail glass.

BOMBAY PUNCH

Juice of 1 Dozen Lemons
Add enough powdered sugar to
sweeten. Place large block of ice in
punch bowl and stir. Then add:
1 qt. Old Mr. Boston Five Star
    Brandy
1 qt. Sherry Wine
¼ pt. Maraschino
¼ pt. Curacao
4 qts. Champagne
2 qts. Carbonated Water
Some prefer to add the strained con-
tents of a pot of tea. Stir well and
decorate with fruits in season. Serve
in 4 oz. Punch glasses.

BOOSTER COCKTAIL

1 Teaspoon Curacao
White of 1 Egg
2 oz. Old Mr. Boston Five Star
    Brandy
Shake well with cracked ice and
strain into 4 oz. cocktail glass. Grate
nutmeg on top.

BOSTON COCKTAIL

¾ oz. Old Mr. Boston Dry Gin
¾ oz. Old Mr. Boston Apricot Fla-
    vored Brandy
Juice of ¼ Lemon
¼ oz. Grenadine
Shake well with cracked ice and
strain into 3 oz. cocktail glass.

BOSTON COOLER

Into 12 oz. Tom Collins glass, put:
Juice ½ Lemon
1 Teaspoon Powdered Sugar
2 oz. Carbonated Water
Stir. Then fill glass with cracked ice
and add:
2 oz. Old Mr. Boston Imported
    Rum
Fill with carbonated water or gin-
ger ale and stir again. Insert spiral
of orange or lemon peel (or both) and
dangle end over rim of glass.

BOSTON SIDE CAR COCKTAIL

¾ oz. Old Mr. Boston Five Star
    Brandy
¾ oz. Old Mr. Boston Imported
    Rum
¾ oz. Triple Sec
Juice ½ Lime
Shake well with cracked ice and
strain into 3 oz. cocktail glass.

B

BOSTON SOUR

Juice ½ Lemon
1 Teaspoon Powdered Sugar
2 oz. Old Mr. Boston Whiskey*
White of 1 Egg
Shake well with cracked ice and strain into 8 oz. highball glass. Then add cube of ice, fill with carbonated water and decorate with half-slice of lemon and a cherry.

BOURBON HIGHBALL

1 Cube of Ice
2 oz. Old Mr. Boston Kentucky
  Bourbon Whiskey
Fill 8 oz. highball glass with ginger ale or carbonated water. Add twist of lemon peel, if desired, and stir.

BRANDY AND SODA

2 Cubes of Ice
2 oz. Old Mr. Boston Five Star
  Brandy
6 oz. Carbonated Water
Serve in 12 oz. Tom Collins glass and stir.

BRANDY BLAZER

1 Lump Sugar
1 Piece Orange Peel
1 Piece Lemon Peel
2 oz. Old Mr. Boston Five Star
  Brandy
Use Old Fashioned cocktail glass. Light with a match, stir with long spoon for a few seconds and strain into a hot whiskey glass.

BRANDY COBBLER

Dissolve: 1 teaspoon powdered sugar in 2 oz. carbonated water; then fill 10 oz. goblet with shaved ice.
Add 2 oz. Old Mr. Boston Five Star
  Brandy
Stir well and decorate with fruits in season. Serve with straws.

BRANDY COCKTAIL

2 oz. Old Mr. Boston Five Star
  Brandy
¼ Teaspoon Simple Syrup
2 Dashes Bitters
Twist of Lemon Peel
Stir well with cracked ice and strain into 3 oz. cocktail glass.

BRANDY COLLINS

Juice ½ Lemon
1 Teaspoon Powdered Sugar
2 oz. Old Mr. Boston Five Star
  Brandy
Shake well with cracked ice and strain into 12 oz. Tom Collins glass. Add several cubes of ice, fill with carbonated water and stir. Decorate with slice of orange, lemon and a cherry. Serve with straws.

13

*Bourbon, Blended, Rye or Canadian.

BRANDY CRUSTA COCKTAIL

Moisten the edge of 4 oz. cocktail glass with lemon and dip into sugar. Cut the rind of half a lemon in a spiral, and place in glass.

1 Teaspoon Maraschino
1 Dash Bitters
1 Teaspoon Lemon Juice
½ oz. Curacao
2 oz. Old Mr. Boston Five Star Brandy

Stir above ingredients in mixing glass and strain into glass prepared as above. Add slice of orange.

BRANDY DAISY

Juice of ½ Lemon
½ Teaspoon Powdered Sugar
1 Teaspoon Raspberry Syrup or Grenadine
2 oz. Old Mr. Boston Five Star Brandy

Shake well with cracked ice and strain into Stein or 8 oz. metal cup. Add cube of ice and decorate with fruit.

BRANDY EGGNOG

1 Egg
1 Teaspoon Powdered Sugar
2 oz. Old Mr. Boston Five Star Brandy
Fill glass with Milk

Shake well with cracked ice and strain into 12 oz. Tom Collins glass. Grate nutmeg on top.

BRANDY FIX

Juice ½ Lemon
1 Teaspoon Powdered Sugar
1 Teaspoon Water
Stir. Then fill glass with shaved ice
2½ oz. Old Mr. Boston Five Star Brandy
Use 8 oz. highball glass. Stir well Add slice of lemon. Serve with straw

BRANDY FIZZ

Juice ½ Lemon
1 Teaspoon Powdered Sugar
2 oz. Old Mr. Boston Five Star Brandy

Shake well with cracked ice and strain into 7 oz. highball glass. Fill with carbonated water.

BRANDY FLIP

1 Egg
1 Teaspoon Powdered Sugar
1½ oz. Old Mr. Boston Five Star Brandy
2 Teaspoons Sweet Cream (if desired)

Shake well with cracked ice and strain into 5 oz. flip glass. Grate little nutmeg on top.

BRANDY GUMP COCKTAIL

1½ oz. Old Mr. Boston Five Star Brandy
Juice of ½ Lemon
½ Teaspoon Grenadine
Shake well with cracked ice and strain into 3 oz. cocktail glass.

14

BRANDY HIGHBALL

1 Cube of Ice
2 oz. Old Mr. Boston Five Star Brandy
Fill 8 oz. highball glass with ginger ale or carbonated water. Add twist of lemon peel, if desired, and stir gently.

BRANDY JULEP

Into 12 oz. Tom Collins glass put:
1 Teaspoon Powdered Sugar
5 or 6 Sprigs Fresh Mint
2½ oz. Old Mr. Boston Five Star Brandy
Then fill glass with finely shaved ice, and stir until mint rises to top, being careful not to bruise mint. (Do not hold glass with hand while stirring.) Decorate with slice of pineapple, orange, lemon and a cherry. Serve with straws.

BRANDY MILK PUNCH

1 Teaspoon Powdered Sugar
2 oz. Old Mr. Boston Five Star Brandy
½ Pint Milk
Shake well with cracked ice, strain into 12 oz. Tom Collins glass and grate nutmeg on top.

BRANDY PUNCH

Juice of 1 Dozen Lemons
Juice of 4 Oranges
Add enough sugar to sweeten.
8 oz. Grenadine
1 qt. Carbonated Water
Place large block of ice in punc bowl and stir well. Then add:
½ Pint Curacao
2 qts. Old Mr. Boston Five St Brandy
Some prefer to add the strained con tents of a pot of tea. Stir well an decorate with fruits in season. Serv in 4 oz. punch glasses.

BRANDY SANGAREE

Dissolve ½ teaspoon powdered suga in 1 teaspoon of water.
2 oz. Old Mr. Boston Five St Brandy
2 Cubes of Ice
Serve in 8 oz. highball glass. Fi balance with soda water. Stir, leav ing enough room on which to float tablespoon of Port Wine. Sprinkl lightly with nutmeg.

BRANDY SLING

Dissolve 1 Teaspoon Powdered Suga in Teaspoon of Water and Juice Lemon.
2 oz. Old Mr. Boston Five St Brandy
2 Cubes of Ice
Serve in Old Fashioned cocktail gla and stir. Twist of lemon peel an drop in glass.

BRANDY SMASH

Muddle 1 Lump of Sugar with
oz. Carbonated Water and
Sprigs of Green Mint
oz. Old Mr. Boston Five Star
Brandy
Add a cube of ice. Stir and decorate
with a slice of Orange and a cherry.
Twist lemon peel on top. Use Old
Fashioned cocktail glass.

BRANDY SOUR

Juice ½ Lemon
½ Teaspoon Powdered Sugar
2 oz. Old Mr. Boston Five Star
Brandy
Shake well with cracked ice and
strain into 6 oz. sour glass. Fill with
carbonated water. Decorate with a
half-slice of lemon and a cherry.

BRANDY SQUIRT

1½ oz. Old Mr. Boston Five Star
Brandy
1 Tablespoon Powdered Sugar
1 Teaspoon Raspberry Syrup or
Grenadine
Shake well with cracked ice and
strain into 8 oz. highball glass and
fill with carbonated water. Decorate
with cubes of pineapple and strawberries.

BRANDY SWIZZLE

Made same as GIN SWIZZLE (see
page 43), using 2 oz. Old Mr. Boston Five Star Brandy.

BRANDY TODDY

Use Old Fashioned cocktail glass.
½ Teaspoon Powdered Sugar
2 Teaspoons Water and stir.
2 oz. Old Mr. Boston Five Star
Brandy
1 Lump of Ice
Stir again and twist lemon peel on
top.

BRANDY TODDY (HOT)

Put lump of sugar into hot whiskey
glass and fill two-thirds with boiling
water. Add 2 oz. Old Mr. Boston
Five Star Brandy. Stir and decorate
with slice of lemon. Grate nutmeg on
top.

BRANDY VERMOUTH COCKTAIL

½ oz. Sweet Vermouth
2 oz. Old Mr. Boston Five Star
Brandy
1 Dash Bitters
Stir well with cracked ice and strain
into 3 oz. cocktail glass.

BRAZIL COCKTAIL

1¼ oz. Dry Vermouth
1¼ oz. Sherry Wine
1 Dash Bitters
¼ Teaspoon Absinthe Substitute
Stir well with cracked ice and strain
into 3 oz. cocktail glass.

BREAKFAST EGGNOG

1 Egg
½ oz. Curacao
2 oz. Old Mr. Boston Apricot Flavored Brandy
Fill glass with milk. Shake well with
cracked ice and strain into 12 oz.
Tom Collins glass. Grate nutmeg on
top.

B

BRIGHTON PUNCH

¾ oz. Old Mr. Boston Whiskey*
¾ oz. Cognac
¾ oz. Benedictine
Juice ½ Orange
Juice ½ Lemon
Shake well and pour into 12 oz. Tom Collins glass filled with shaved ice. Then fill with carbonated water and stir gently. Serve with straws. Old Mr. Boston Five Star Brandy may be substituted for Cognac.

BROKEN SPUR COCKTAIL

¾ oz. Sweet Vermouth
1½ oz. Port Wine
¼ Teaspoon Curacao
Stir well with cracked ice and strain into 3 oz. cocktail glass.

BRONX COCKTAIL

1 oz. Old Mr. Boston Dry Gin
½ oz. Dry Vermouth
½ oz. Sweet Vermouth
Juice ¼ Orange
Shake well with cracked ice and strain into 3 oz. cocktail glass. Serve with slice of orange.

BRONX COCKTAIL (DRY)

1 oz. Old Mr. Boston Dry Gin
1 oz. Dry Vermouth
Juice ¼ Orange
Shake well with cracked ice and strain into 3 oz. cocktail glass. Serve with slice of orange.

BRONX GOLDEN COCKTAIL

Made same as BRONX COCKTAIL, *adding the yolk of one egg. Use 4 oz. cocktail glass.*

BRONX SILVER COCKTAIL

Juice of ¼ Orange
White of 1 Egg
½ oz. Dry Vermouth
1 oz. Old Mr. Boston Dry Gin
Shake well with cracked ice and strain into 4 oz. cocktail glass.

BRONX TERRACE COCKTAIL

1½ oz. Old Mr. Boston Dry Gin
1½ oz. Dry Vermouth
Juice of ½ Lime
Shake well with cracked ice and strain into 3 oz. cocktail glass. Add cherry.

BROWN COCKTAIL

¾ oz. Old Mr. Boston Dry Gin
¾ oz. Old Mr. Boston Imported Rum
¾ oz. Dry Vermouth
Stir well with cracked ice and strain into 3 oz. cocktail glass.

BUCKS FIZZ

¼ Glass Orange Juice
Fill with Champagne. Use 12 oz. Tom Collins glass and stir very gently.

BULLDOG COCKTAIL

1¼ oz. Old Mr. Boston Wild Cherry Flavored Brandy
¾ oz. Old Mr. Boston Dry Gin
Juice of ½ Lime
Shake well with cracked ice and strain into 3 oz. cocktail glass.

BULLDOG HIGHBALL

1 Cube of Ice
Juice of ½ Orange
2 oz. Old Mr. Boston Dry Gin
Fill 8 oz. highball glass with ginger ale and stir.

18   * Bourbon, Blended, Rye or Canadian.

BULL'S EYE

1 oz. Old Mr. Boston Five Star
  Brandy
2 oz. Hard Cider
1 Cube of Ice
*Fill 8 oz. highball glass with ginger
ale and stir.*

BULL'S MILK

1 Teaspoon Powdered Sugar
1 oz. Old Mr. Boston Imported
  Rum
1½ oz. Old Mr. Boston Five Star
  Brandy
½ Pint Milk
*Shake well with cracked ice and
strain into 12 oz. Tom Collins glass.
Grate nutmeg and pinch of cinnamon on top.*

BURGUNDY BISHOP

Juice ¼ Lemon
1 Teaspoon Powdered Sugar
1 oz. Old Mr. Boston Imported
  Rum
*Shake well and strain into 8 oz.
highball glass and fill with Burgundy and stir. Decorate with fruits*

BUTTON HOOK COCKTAIL

½ oz. Old Mr. Boston Creme de
  Menthe (White)
½ oz. Old Mr. Boston Apricot Flavored Brandy
½ oz. Absinthe Substitute
½ oz. Old Mr. Boston Five Star
  Brandy
*Shake well with cracked ice and
strain into 3 oz. cocktail glass.*

CABARET COCKTAIL

1½ oz. Old Mr. Boston Dry Gin
2 Dashes Bitters
½ Teaspoon Dry Vermouth
¼ Teaspoon Benedictine
*Stir well with cracked ice and strain
into 3 oz. cocktail glass. Serve with a
cherry.*

CABLEGRAM HIGHBALL

Juice ½ Lemon
1 Teaspoon Powdered Sugar
2 oz. Old Mr. Boston Whiskey*
*Stir well with cracked ice and fill
with ginger ale. Use 8 oz. highball
glass.*

* *Bourbon, Blended, Rye or Canadian*

C

CAFÉ DE PARIS COCKTAIL

White of 1 Egg
1 Teaspoon Absinthe Substitute
1 Teaspoon Sweet Cream
1½ oz. Old Mr. Boston Dry Gin
Shake well with cracked ice and strain into 4 oz. cocktail glass.

CAFÉ ROYALE

1 Cup Hot Black Coffee
Put cube of sugar, well soaked with Old Mr. Boston Five Star Brandy, in teaspoon and hold so that it will rest on top of coffee and ignite and hold until flame burns out. Drop contents in coffee.

CALIFORNIA LEMONADE

Juice 1 Lemon
Juice 1 Lime
3 Teaspoons Powdered Sugar
2 oz. Old Mr. Boston Whiskey*
¼ Teaspoon Grenadine
Shake well with cracked ice and strain into 12 oz. Tom Collins glass filled with shaved ice. Fill with carbonated water and decorate with slice of orange, lemon, and a cherry. Serve with straws.

CAMERON'S KICK COCKTAIL

¾ oz. Old Mr. Boston Scotch Whisky
¾ oz. Irish Whiskey
Juice ¼ Lemon
2 Dashes Orange Bitters
Shake well with cracked ice and strain into 3 oz. cocktail glass.

CANADIAN COCKTAIL

1½ oz. Old Mr. Boston Canadian Whisky
¼ Teaspoon Curacao
2 Dashes Bitters
1 Teaspoon Powdered Sugar
Shake well with cracked ice and strain into 3 oz. cocktail glass.

CARDINAL PUNCH

Juice of 1 Dozen Lemons
Add enough Powdered Sugar to sweeten. Place large block of ice in punch bowl and stir well. Then add:
1 pt. Old Mr. Boston Five Star Brandy
1 pt. Old Mr. Boston Imported Rum
1 pt. Champagne
2 qts. Claret
1 qt. Carbonated Water
½ pt. Sweet Vermouth
Some prefer to add the strained contents of a pot of tea. Stir well and decorate with fruits in season. Serve in 4 oz. punch glasses.

CARROL COCKTAIL

1½ oz. Old Mr. Boston Five Star Brandy
¾ oz. Sweet Vermouth
Stir well with cracked ice and strain into 3 oz. cocktail glass. Serve with a cherry.

21

Bourbon, Blended, Rye or Canadian.

CASINO COCKTAIL

2 Dashes Orange Bitters
¼ Teaspoon Maraschino
¼ Teaspoon Lemon Juice
2 oz. Old Mr. Boston Dry Gin
Shake well with cracked ice and strain into 3 oz. cocktail glass. Serve with a cherry.

CHAMPAGNE COCKTAIL

Spiral Rind of ½ Lemon
1 Lump Sugar
2 Dashes Bitters
Use 6 oz. Champagne glass. Fill with Champagne.

CHAMPAGNE CUP

Use Large Glass Pitcher
4 Teaspoons Powdered Sugar
6 oz. Carbonated Water
½ oz. Triple Sec
½ oz. Curacao
2 oz. Old Mr. Boston Five Star Brandy
Fill pitcher with cubes of ice. Add 1 pint of Champagne. Stir well and decorate with as many fruits as available and also rind of cucumber inserted on each side of pitcher. Top with small bunch of mint sprigs. Serve in 5 oz. claret glass.

CHAMPAGNE PUNCH

Juice of 1 Dozen Lemons
Add enough Powdered Sugar to sweeten. Place large block of ice in punch bowl and stir well. Then add
½ pt. Maraschino
½ pt. Curacao
1 pt. Old Mr. Boston Five Star Brandy
2 qts. Champagne
1 qt. Carbonated Water
Some prefer to add the strained contents of a pot of tea. Stir well and decorate with fruits in season. Serve in 4 oz. punch glasses.

CHAMPAGNE VELVET

See BLACK VELVET on page 9.

CHAMPS ÉLYSÉES COCKTAIL

1 oz. Cognac
½ oz. Yellow Chartreuse
Juice of ¼ Lemon
½ Teaspoon Powdered Sugar
1 Dash Bitters
Shake well with cracked ice and strain into 3 oz. cocktail glass. Old Mr. Boston Five Star Brandy may be substituted for Cognac.

CHARLES COCKTAIL

1¼ oz. Sweet Vermouth
1¼ oz. Old Mr. Boston Five Star Brandy
1 Dash Bitters
Stir well with cracked ice and strain into 3 oz. cocktail glass.

Chelsea Side Car Cocktail

Juice of ¼ Lemon
¾ oz. Triple Sec
¾ oz. Old Mr. Boston Dry Gin
Shake well with cracked ice and strain into 3 oz. cocktail glass.

Cherry Blossom Cocktail

1 oz. Old Mr. Boston Wild Cherry Flavored Brandy
1 oz. Old Mr. Boston Five Star Brandy
¼ Teaspoon Curacao
¼ Teaspoon Lemon Juice
¼ Teaspoon Grenadine
Shake well with cracked ice and strain into 3 oz. cocktail glass.

Cherry Fizz

Juice ½ Lemon
2 oz. Old Mr. Boston Wild Cherry Flavored Brandy
Shake well with cracked ice and strain into 7 oz. highball glass. Fill with carbonated water and decorate with a cherry.

Cherry Flip

1 Egg
1 Teaspoon Powdered Sugar
1½ oz. Old Mr. Boston Wild Cherry Flavored Brandy
2 Teaspoons Sweet Cream (if desired)
Shake well with cracked ice and strain into 5 oz. flip glass. Grate a little nutmeg on top.

Cherry Sling

2 Cubes of Ice
2 oz. Old Mr. Boston Wild Cherry Flavored Brandy
Juice ½ Lemon
Serve in Old Fashioned cocktail glass and stir. Twist of lemon peel and drop in glass.

Chicago Cocktail

2 oz. Old Mr. Boston Five Star Brandy
1 Dash Bitters
¼ Teaspoon Curacao
Stir well with cracked ice and strain into 3 oz. cocktail glass. Frost glass by rubbing slice of lemon around rim and then dip in powdered sugar.

Chicago Fizz

Juice ½ Lemon
1 Teaspoon Powdered Sugar
White of 1 Egg
1 oz. Port Wine
1 oz. Old Mr. Boston Imported Rum
Shake well with cracked ice and strain into 7 oz. highball glass. Fill with carbonated water and stir.

Chinese Cocktail

½ oz. Grenadine
1½ oz. Jamaica Rum
1 Dash Bitters
1 Teaspoon Maraschino
1 Teaspoon Curacao
Shake well with cracked ice and strain into 3 oz. cocktail glass.

CHOCOLATE COCKTAIL

1½ oz. Port Wine
¼ oz. Yellow Chartreuse
Yolk of 1 Egg
1 Teaspoon Powdered Sugar
Shake well with cracked ice and strain into 4 oz. cocktail glass.

CHOCOLATE DAISY

Juice ½ Lemon
½ Teaspoon Powdered Sugar
1 Teaspoon Raspberry Syrup or Grenadine
1½ oz. Old Mr. Boston Five Star Brandy
1½ oz. Port Wine
Shake well with cracked ice and strain into stein or 8 oz. metal cup. Add cube of ice and decorate with fruit.

CHOCOLATE FLIP

1 Egg
1 Teaspoon of Powdered Sugar
¾ oz. Old Mr. Boston Sloe Gin
¾ oz. Old Mr. Boston Five Star Brandy
2 Teaspoons Sweet Cream (if desired)
Shake well with cracked ice and strain into 5 oz. flip glass. Grate a little nutmeg on top.

CHOCOLATE SOLDIER COCKTAIL

Juice ½ Lime
¾ oz. Dubonnet
1½ oz. Old Mr. Boston Dry Gin
Shake well with cracked ice and strain into 3 oz. cocktail glass.

CHRISTMAS YULE EGGNOG

Beat the yolks and whites of 1 Dozen Eggs separately and then pour together and add:
1 Pinch Baking Soda
6 oz. Old Mr. Boston Imported Rum
2 lbs. Granulated Sugar
Beat into stiff batter. Then add:
1 qt. Milk
1 qt. Sweet Cream
2 qts. Old Mr. Boston Whiskey
Stir. Set in refrigerator over night. Before serving, stir again, and serve in 4 oz. punch glasses, and grate nutmeg on top.

CIDER CUP

Use Large Glass Pitcher
4 Teaspoons Powdered Sugar
6 oz. Carbonated Water
½ oz. Triple Sec
½ oz. Curacao
2 oz. Old Mr. Boston Five Star Brandy
Fill pitcher with cubes of ice. Add pint of cider. Stir well and decorate with as many fruits as available and also rind of cucumber inserted each side of pitcher. Top with small bunch of mint sprigs. Serve in 5 oz. claret glasses.

CIDER EGGNOG

1 Egg
1 Teaspoon Powdered Sugar
¼ pt. Milk
Shake well with cracked ice and strain into 12 oz. Tom Collins glass. Then fill glass with sweet cider and stir. Grate nutmeg on top.

* *Bourbon, Blended, Rye or Canadian*

CIRCUS RICKEY

Cube of Ice
Juice ½ Lime
2 Teaspoon Grenadine
½ oz. Old Mr. Boston Dry Gin
Fill 8 oz. highball glass with carbonated water and stir. Leave lime in glass.

CLARET COBBLER

Dissolve: 1 teaspoon powdered sugar in 2 oz. carbonated water; then add 2 oz. Claret. Fill 10 oz. goblet with shaved ice and stir. Decorate with fruits in season. Serve with straws.

CLARET CUP

Use Large Glass Pitcher
2 Teaspoons Powdered Sugar
2 oz. Carbonated Water
1 oz. Triple Sec
1 oz. Curacao
2 oz. Old Mr. Boston Five Star Brandy
Fill pitcher with cubes of ice. Add 1 pint of Claret. Stir well and decorate with as many fruits as available and also rind of cucumber inserted on each side of pitcher. Top with small bunch of mint sprigs. Serve in 5 oz. claret glass.

CLARET PUNCH

Juice of 1 Dozen Lemons
Add enough powdered sugar to sweeten. Place large block of ice in punch bowl and stir well. Then add:
½ pt. Curacao
1 pt. Old Mr. Boston Five Star Brandy
3 qts. Claret
1 qt. Carbonated Water
Some prefer to add the strained contents of a pot of tea. Stir well and decorate with fruits in season. Serve in 4 oz. punch glasses.

CLARIDGE COCKTAIL

¾ oz. Old Mr. Boston Dry Gin
¾ oz. Dry Vermouth
½ oz. Old Mr. Boston Apricot Flavored Brandy
½ oz. Triple Sec
Stir well with cracked ice and strain into 3 oz. cocktail glass.

CLASSIC COCKTAIL

Juice of ¼ Lemon
¼ oz. Curacao
¼ oz. Maraschino
1 oz. Old Mr. Boston Five Star Brandy
Shake well with cracked ice and strain into 3 oz. cocktail glass. Frost rim of glass by rubbing with lemon and dipping in powdered sugar.

CLOVE COCKTAIL

1 oz. Sweet Vermouth
½ oz. Old Mr. Boston Sloe Gin
½ oz. Muscatel Wine
Stir well with cracked ice and strain into 3 oz. cocktail glass.

CLOVER CLUB COCKTAIL

Juice ½ Lemon
2 Teaspoons Grenadine
White of 1 Egg
1½ oz. Old Mr. Boston Dry Gin
Shake well with cracked ice and strain into 4 oz. cocktail glass.

CLOVER LEAF COCKTAIL

Juice 1 Lime
2 Teaspoons Grenadine
White of 1 Egg
1½ oz. Old Mr. Boston Dry Gin
Shake well with cracked ice and strain into 4 oz. cocktail glass. Serve with mint leaf on top.

CLUB COCKTAIL

1½ oz. Old Mr. Boston Dry Gin
¾ oz. Sweet Vermouth
Stir well with cracked ice and strain into 3 oz. cocktail glass. Add a cherry or olive.

COBBLERS

See Index on page 139 for complete list of COBBLER *recipes.*

COFFEE COCKTAIL

1 Egg
1 Teaspoon Powdered Sugar
1 oz. Port Wine
1 oz. Old Mr. Boston Five Star Brandy
Shake well with cracked ice and strain into 5 oz. cocktail glass. Grate nutmeg on top.

COFFEE FLIP

1 Egg
1 Teaspoon Powdered Sugar
1 oz. Old Mr. Boston Five St Brandy
1 oz. Port Wine
2 Teaspoons Sweet Cream (if desired)
Shake well with cracked ice a strain into 5 oz. flip glass. Grate little nutmeg on top.

COGNAC HIGHBALL

1 Cube of Ice
2 oz. Cognac
Fill 8 oz. highball glass with ging ale or carbonated water. Add tw of lemon peel, if desired, and s gently.

COLD DECK COCKTAIL

½ oz. Old Mr. Boston Creme Menthe (White)
½ oz. Sweet Vermouth
1 oz. Old Mr. Boston Five S Brandy
Stir well with cracked ice and str into 3 oz. cocktail glass.

COLLINS

See Index on page 139 for compl list of COLLINS *recipes.*

COLONIAL COCKTAIL

½ oz. Grapefruit Juice
1 Teaspoon Maraschino
1½ oz. Old Mr. Boston Dry Gin
Shake well with cracked ice a strain into 3 oz. cocktail glass. Se with an olive.

COMMODORE COCKTAIL

Juice ½ Lime or ¼ Lemon
1 Teaspoon Powdered Sugar
2 Dashes Orange Bitters
1½ oz. Old Mr. Boston Whiskey*
Shake well with cracked ice and strain into 3 oz. cocktail glass.

COOLERS

See Index on page 140 for complete list of COOLER recipes.

COOPERSTOWN COCKTAIL

½ oz. Dry Vermouth
½ oz. Sweet Vermouth
1 oz. Old Mr. Boston Dry Gin
2 Sprigs Fresh Mint
Shake well with cracked ice and strain into 3 oz. cocktail glass.

CORNELL COCKTAIL

½ Teaspoon Lemon Juice
1 Teaspoon Maraschino
White of 1 Egg
1½ oz. Old Mr. Boston Dry Gin
Shake well with cracked ice and strain into 4 oz. cocktail glass.

CORONATION COCKTAIL

¾ oz. Old Mr. Boston Dry Gin
¾ oz. Dubonnet
¾ oz. Dry Vermouth
Stir well with cracked ice and strain into 3 oz. cocktail glass.

COUNTRY CLUB COOLER

Into 12 oz. Tom Collins glass, put:
½ Teaspoon Grenadine
2 oz. Carbonated Water *and stir.*
Fill glass with cracked ice and add:
2 oz. Dry Vermouth
Fill with carbonated water or ginger ale and stir again. Insert spiral of orange or lemon peel (or both) and dangle end over rim of glass.

COWBOY COCKTAIL

1½ oz. Old Mr. Boston Whiskey*
½ oz. Sweet Cream
Shake well with cracked ice and strain into 3 oz. cocktail glass.

CREAM FIZZ

Juice ½ Lemon
1 Teaspoon Powdered Sugar
2 oz. Old Mr. Boston Dry Gin
1 Teaspoon Fresh Cream
Shake well with cracked ice and strain into 8 oz. highball glass. Fill with carbonated water and stir.

CREAM PUFF

2 oz. Old Mr. Boston Imported Rum
1 oz. Sweet Cream
½ Teaspoon Powdered Sugar
Shake well with cracked ice and strain into 8 oz. highball glass. Fill with carbonated water and stir.

* *Bourbon, Blended, Rye or Canadian*

C

CREME DE GIN COCKTAIL

1½ oz. Old Mr. Boston Dry Gin
½ oz. Old Mr. Boston Creme de
  Menthe (white)
White of 1 Egg
2 Teaspoons Lemon Juice
2 Teaspoons Orange Juice
*Shake well with cracked ice and
strain into 4 oz. cocktail glass.*

CREME DE MENTHE FRAPPE

*Fill cocktail glass up to brim with
shaved ice. Add Old Mr. Boston
Creme de Menthe (green). Serve
with two short straws.*

CREOLE LADY COCKTAIL

1¼ oz. Old Mr. Boston Whiskey*
1¼ oz. Madeira Wine
1 Teaspoon Grenadine
*Stir well with cracked ice and strain
into 3 oz. cocktail glass. Serve with 1
green and 1 red cherry.*

CRIMSON COCKTAIL

1½ oz. Old Mr. Boston Dry Gin
2 Teaspoons Lemon Juice
1 Teaspoon Grenadine
*Shake well with cracked ice and
strain into 3 oz. cocktail glass, leaving enough room on top to float ¾ oz.
Port Wine.*

CRYSTAL SLIPPER COCKTAIL

½ oz. Creme de Yvette
2 Dashes Orange Bitters
1½ oz. Old Mr. Boston Dry Gin
*Stir well with cracked ice and strain
into 3 oz. cocktail glass.*

CUBA LIBRE

Juice ½ Lime
Drop rind in glass.
2 oz. Old Mr. Boston Imported
  Rum
2 Cubes of Ice
*Fill glass with any cola. Use 10 oz.
glass and stir well.*

CUBAN COCKTAIL No. 1

Juice of ½ Lime
½ Teaspoon Powdered Sugar
2 oz. Old Mr. Boston Imported
  Rum
*Shake well with cracked ice and
strain into 3 oz. cocktail glass.*

CUBAN COCKTAIL No. 2

Juice of ½ Lime or ¼ Lemon
½ oz. Old Mr. Boston Apricot
  Flavored Brandy
1½ oz. Old Mr. Boston Five Star
  Brandy
1 Teaspoon Old Mr. Boston
  Imported Rum
*Shake well with cracked ice and
strain into 3 oz. cocktail glass.*

CUBAN SPECIAL COCKTAIL

½ oz. Pineapple Juice
Juice ½ Lime
1 oz. Old Mr. Boston Imported
  Rum
½ Teaspoon Curacao
*Shake well with cracked ice and
strain into 3 oz. cocktail glass. Decorate with stick of pineapple and a
cherry.*

CUPS

*See Index on page 140 for complete
list of CUP recipes.*

* *Bourbon, Blended, Rye or Canadian.*

D

DAIQUIRI COCKTAIL

Juice 1 Lime
1 Teaspoon Powdered Sugar
1½ oz. Old Mr. Boston Imported
    Rum
*Shake well with cracked ice and
strain into 3 oz. cocktail glass.*

DAISIES

*See Index on page 141 for complete
list of* DAISY *recipes.*

DAMN-THE-WEATHER
COCKTAIL

1 Teaspoon Curacao
½ oz. Orange Juice
½ oz. Sweet Vermouth
1 oz. Old Mr. Boston Dry Gin
*Shake well with cracked ice and
strain into 3 oz. cocktail glass.*

DARB COCKTAIL

1 Teaspoon Lemon Juice
¾ oz. Dry Vermouth
¾ oz. Old Mr. Boston Dry Gin
¾ oz. Old Mr. Boston Apricot
    Flavored Brandy
*Shake well with cracked ice and
strain into 3 oz. cocktail glass.*

DEAUVILLE COCKTAIL

Juice of ¼ Lemon
½ oz. Old Mr. Boston Five Sta
    Brandy
½ oz. Apple Brandy
½ oz. Triple Sec
*Shake well with cracked ice an
strain into 3 oz. cocktail glass.*

DEEP SEA COCKTAIL

1 oz. Dry Vermouth
¼ Teaspoon Absinthe Substitute
1 Dash Orange Bitters
1 oz. Old Mr. Boston Dry Gin
*Stir well with cracked ice and strai
into 3 oz. cocktail glass.*

DEMPSEY COCKTAIL

1 oz. Old Mr. Boston Dry Gin
1 oz. Apple Brandy
½ Teaspoon Absinthe Substitute
½ Teaspoon Grenadine
*Stir well with cracked ice and strain
into 3 oz. cocktail glass.*

DERBY FIZZ

Juice ½ Lemon
1 Teaspoon Powdered Sugar
1 Egg
2 oz. Old Mr. Boston Scotch
  Whisky
1 Teaspoon Curacao
*Shake well with cracked ice and
strain into 8 oz. highball glass. Fill
with carbonated water and stir.*

DEVIL'S COCKTAIL

½ Teaspoon Lemon Juice
1¼ oz. Port Wine
1¼ oz. Dry Vermouth
*Stir well with cracked ice and strain
into 3 oz. cocktail glass.*

DIAMOND FIZZ

Juice ½ Lemon
1 Teaspoon Powdered Sugar
2 oz. Old Mr. Boston Dry Gin
*Shake well with cracked ice and
strain into 7 oz. highball glass. Fill
with champagne and stir gently.*

DIANA COCKTAIL

Fill 3 oz. cocktail glass with shaved
ice, then fill ¾ full with Old Mr.
Boston Creme de Menthe (white)
and float Old Mr. Boston Five Star
Brandy on top.

DILLATINI COCKTAIL

See *Special Martini Section* on
pages 116 and 117.

DINAH COCKTAIL

Juice of ¼ Lemon
½ Teaspoon Powdered Sugar
½ oz. Old Mr. Boston Whiskey*
2 or 3 Sprigs Fresh Mint
*Shake very well with cracked ice and
strain into 3 oz. cocktail glass. Serve
with a mint leaf.*

DIPLOMAT COCKTAIL

1½ oz. Dry Vermouth
½ oz. Sweet Vermouth
2 Dashes Bitters
½ Teaspoon Maraschino
*Stir well with cracked ice and strain
into 3 oz. cocktail glass. Serve with
½ slice of lemon and a cherry.*

DIXIE COCKTAIL

Juice of ¼ Orange
½ oz. Absinthe Substitute
½ oz. Dry Vermouth
1 oz. Old Mr. Boston Dry Gin
*Shake well with cracked ice and
strain into 4 oz. cocktail glass.*

DIXIE JULEP

Into a 12 oz. Tom Collins glass put
4 Sprigs of Mint
1 Teaspoon Powdered Sugar
2½ oz. Old Mr. Boston Kentucky
  Bourbon Whiskey
*Fill with shaved ice and stir gently
until glass is frosted. Decorate with
sprigs of mint. Serve with straws.*

DIXIE WHISKEY COCKTAIL

½ Lump of Sugar
1 Dash Bitters
¼ Teaspoon Curacao
½ Teaspoon Old Mr. Boston
  Creme de Menthe (white)
2 oz. Old Mr. Boston Whiskey*
*Shake well with cracked ice and
strain into 3 oz. cocktail glass.*

31

* *Bourbon, Blended, Rye or Canadian.*

DOUBLE STANDARD SOUR

Juice ½ Lemon or 1 Lime
½ Teaspoon Powdered Sugar
¾ oz. Old Mr. Boston Whiskey*
¾ oz. Old Mr. Boston Dry Gin
½ Teaspoon Raspberry Syrup or
    Grenadine
*Shake well with cracked ice and
strain into 6 oz. sour glass. Fill with
carbonated water. Decorate with a
half-slice of lemon and a cherry.*

DREAM COCKTAIL

¾ oz. Curacao
1½ oz. Old Mr. Boston Five Star
    Brandy
¼ Teaspoon Old Mr. Boston
    Anisette
*Shake well with cracked ice and
strain into 3 oz. cocktail glass.*

DRY MARTINI COCKTAIL

See *Special Martini Section* on
pages 116 and 117.

DU BARRY COCKTAIL

1 Dash Bitters
¾ oz. Dry Vermouth
½ Teaspoon Absinthe Substitute
1½ oz. Old Mr. Boston Dry Gin
*Stir well with cracked ice and strain
into 3 oz. cocktail glass. Add slice of
orange.*

DUBONNET COCKTAIL

1½ oz. Dubonnet
¾ oz. Old Mr. Boston Dry Gin
1 Dash Orange Bitters *if desired.*
*Stir well with cracked ice and strain
into 3 oz. cocktail glass. Twist of
lemon peel on top and drop in glass.*

DUBONNET FIZZ

Juice ½ Orange
Juice ¼ Lemon
1 Teaspoon Old Mr. Boston Wil•
    Cherry Flavored Brandy
2 oz. Dubonnet
*Shake well with cracked ice an•
strain into 7 oz. highball glass. Fi•
with carbonated water and stir.*

DUBONNET HIGHBALL

1 Cube of Ice
2 oz. Dubonnet
*Fill 8 oz. highball glass with ginge•
ale or carbonated water. Add twi•
of lemon peel, if desired, and stir.*

DUCHESS COCKTAIL

¾ oz. Dry Vermouth
¾ oz. Sweet Vermouth
¾ oz. Absinthe Substitute
*Stir well with cracked ice and stra•
into 3 oz. cocktail glass.*

DUKE COCKTAIL

½ oz. Triple Sec
1 Teaspoon Orange Juice
2 Teaspoons Lemon Juice
½ Teaspoon Maraschino
1 Egg
*Shake well with cracked ice an•
strain into 8 oz. stem glass. Fill w•
Champagne and stir very gently.*

* Bourbon, Blended, Rye or Canadi•

EAST INDIA COCKTAIL No. 1

½ oz. Old Mr. Boston Five Star
  Brandy
½ Teaspoon Pineapple Juice
½ Teaspoon Curacao
  Teaspoon Jamaica Rum
  Dash Bitters
*Shake well with cracked ice and
strain into 3 oz. cocktail glass. Twist
of lemon peel and add a cherry.*

EAST INDIA COCKTAIL No. 2

¼ oz. Dry Vermouth
¼ oz. Sherry Wine
  Dash Orange Bitters
*Stir well with cracked ice and strain
into 3 oz. cocktail glass.*

ECLIPSE COCKTAIL

  oz. Old Mr. Boston Dry Gin
  oz. Old Mr. Boston Sloe Gin
½ Teaspoon Lemon Juice
*Put enough grenadine into 4 oz.
cocktail glass to cover a ripe olive.
Mix the above ingredients in ice and
pour gently onto the grenadine so
that they do not mix.*

EGGNOGS

*See Special Eggnog Section on pages
14 and 115 and also Index on
page 143 for complete list of EGG-
NOG recipes.*

EGG SOUR

1 Egg
1 Teaspoon Powdered Sugar
Juice ½ Lemon
2 oz. Old Mr. Boston Five Star
  Brandy
¼ Teaspoon Curacao
*Shake well with cracked ice and
strain into 8 oz. highball glass.*

EL PRESIDENTE COCKTAIL
No. 1

Juice 1 Lime
1 Teaspoon Pineapple Juice
1 Teaspoon Grenadine
1½ oz. Old Mr. Boston Imported
  Rum
*Shake well with cracked ice and
strain into 3 oz. cocktail glass.*

EL PRESIDENTE COCKTAIL
No. 2

¾ oz. Dry Vermouth
1½ oz. Old Mr. Boston Imported
  Rum
1 Dash Bitters
*Stir well with cracked ice and strain
into 3 oz. cocktail glass.*

E

ELK'S OWN COCKTAIL

White of 1 Egg
1½ oz. Old Mr. Boston Whiskey*
¾ oz. Port Wine
Juice ¼ Lemon
1 Teaspoon Powdered Sugar
*Add a strip of Pineapple. Shake well
with cracked ice and strain into 4 oz.
cocktail glass.*

EMERALD ISLE COCKTAIL

2 oz. Old Mr. Boston Dry Gin
1 Teaspoon Old Mr. Boston
  Creme de Menthe (Green)
3 Dashes Bitters
*Stir well with crackèd ice and strain
into 3 oz. cocktail glass.*

ENGLISH HIGHBALL

1 Cube of Ice
¾ oz. Old Mr. Boston Dry Gin
¾ oz. Old Mr. Boston Five Star
  Brandy
¾ oz. Sweet Vermouth
*Fill 8 oz. highball glass with ginger
ale or carbonated water. Add twist
of lemon peel, if desired, and stir.*

ENGLISH ROSE COCKTAIL

1¼ oz. Old Mr. Boston Dry Gin
¾ oz. Old Mr. Boston Apricot
  Flavored Brandy
¾ oz. Dry Vermouth
1 Teaspoon Grenadine
¼ Teaspoon Lemon Juice
*Shake well with cracked ice and
strain into 4 oz. cocktail glass. Frost
rim of glass by rubbing with lemon
and dipping in sugar. Serve with a
cherry.*

ETHEL DUFFY COCKTAIL

¾ oz. Old Mr. Boston Apricot
  Flavored Brandy
¾ oz. Old Mr. Boston Creme d
  Menthe (White)
¾ oz. Curacao
*Shake well with cracked ice ar
strain into 3 oz. cocktail glass.*

EVERYBODY'S IRISH COCKTAIL

1 Teaspoon Old Mr. Boston
  Creme de Menthe (Green)
1 Teaspoon Green Chartreuse
2 oz. Irish Whiskey
*Stir well with cracked ice and stra
into 3 oz. cocktail glass. Serve wi
green olive.*

EYE-OPENER COCKTAIL

Yolk of 1 Egg
½ Teaspoon Powdered Sugar
1 Teaspoon Absinthe Substitute
1 Teaspoon Curacao
1 Teaspoon Old Mr. Boston
  Creme de Cacao
2 oz. Old Mr. Boston Imported
  Rum
*Shake well with cracked ice ar
strain into 4 oz. cocktail glass.*

34

* Bourbon, Blended, Rye or Canad

Old Mr. Boston

PRODUCT OF SCOTLAND

BLENDED
SCOTCH
WHISKY

100% SCOTCH WHISKIES
THIS IS TRULY THE MILDEST SCOTCH WHISKY
MADE FROM CHOICE HIGHLAND STOCKS

EIGHTY SIX PROOF • FOUR-FIFTHS QUART
DISTILLED AND BLENDED IN SCOTLAND • IMPORTED AND BOTTLED BY
MR. BOSTON DISTILLER INC., BOSTON, MASSACHUSETTS

Eighty Six Proof

IMPORTED

Fair and Warmer Cocktail

¾ oz. Sweet Vermouth
1½ oz. Old Mr. Boston Imported
    Rum
½ Teaspoon Curacao
*Stir well with cracked ice and strain
into 3 oz. cocktail glass.*

Fairy Belle Cocktail

White of 1 Egg
1 Teaspoon Grenadine
¾ oz. Old Mr. Boston Apricot
    Flavored Brandy
1½ oz. Old Mr. Boston Dry Gin
*Shake well with cracked ice and
strain into 4 oz. cocktail glass.*

Fallen Angel Cocktail

Juice of 1 Lemon or ½ Lime
1½ oz. Old Mr. Boston Dry Gin
1 Dash Bitters
½ Teaspoon Old Mr. Boston Creme
    de Menthe (white)
*Shake well with cracked ice and
strain into 3 oz. cocktail glass. Serve
with a cherry.*

Fancy Brandy Cocktail

2 oz. Old Mr. Boston Five Star
    Brandy
1 Dash Bitters
¼ Teaspoon Curacao
¼ Teaspoon Powdered Sugar
*Shake well with cracked ice and
strain into 3 oz. cocktail glass. Twist
of lemon peel and drop in glass.*

Fancy Gin Cocktail

Same as Fancy Brandy Cocktail
except substitute: 2 oz. Old Mr. Boston Dry Gin

Fancy Whiskey Cocktail

Same as Fancy Brandy Cocktail
except substitute: 2 oz. Old Mr. Boston Whiskey*

Fantasio Cocktail

1 Teaspoon Old Mr. Boston Creme
    de Menthe (White)
1 Teaspoon Maraschino
1 oz. Old Mr. Boston Five Star
    Brandy
¾ oz. Dry Vermouth
*Stir well with cracked ice and strain
into 3 oz. cocktail glass.*

* Bourbon, Blended, Rye or Canadian.

FARMER'S COCKTAIL

1 oz. Old Mr. Boston Dry Gin
½ oz. Dry Vermouth
½ oz. Sweet Vermouth
2 Dashes Bitters
Stir well with cracked ice and strain into 3 oz. cocktail glass.

FAVOURITE COCKTAIL

¾ oz. Old Mr. Boston Apricot Flavored Brandy
¾ oz. Dry Vermouth
¾ oz. Old Mr. Boston Dry Gin
¼ Teaspoon Lemon Juice
Shake well with cracked ice and strain into 3 oz. cocktail glass.

FIFTH AVENUE

⅓ oz. Old Mr. Boston Creme de Cacao
⅓ oz. Old Mr. Boston Apricot Flavored Brandy
⅓ oz. Sweet Cream
Pour carefully, in order given, into Pousse Café glass, so that each ingredient floats on preceding one.

FIFTY-FIFTY COCKTAIL

1¼ oz. Old Mr. Boston Dry Gin
1¼ oz. Dry Vermouth
Stir well with cracked ice and strain into 3 oz. cocktail glass.

FINE AND DANDY COCKTAIL

Juice of ¼ Lemon
½ oz. Triple Sec
1¼ oz. Old Mr. Boston Dry Gin
1 Dash Bitters
Shake well with cracked ice and strain into 3 oz. cocktail glass. Serve with a cherry.

FIREMAN'S SOUR

Juice 2 Limes
½ Teaspoon Powdered Sugar
½ oz. Grenadine
2 oz. Old Mr. Boston Imported Rum
Shake well with cracked ice and strain into Delmonico glass. Fill with carbonated water, if desired. Decorate with a half-slice of lemon and a cherry.

FISH HOUSE PUNCH

Juice of 1 Dozen Lemons
Add enough Powdered Sugar to sweeten. Place large block of ice in punch bowl and stir well. Then add:
1½ qts. Old Mr. Boston Five Star Brandy
1 pt. Old Mr. Boston Peach Flavored Brandy
1 pt. Old Mr. Boston Imported Rum
1 qt. Carbonated Water
Some prefer to add the strained contents of a pot of tea. Stir well and decorate with fruits in season. Serve in 4 oz. Punch glasses.

FIXES

See Index on page 143 for complete list of FIX recipes.

FIZZES

See Index on page 143 for complete list of FIZZ recipes.

FLAMINGO COCKTAIL

Juice of ½ Lime
½ oz. Old Mr. Boston Apricot Flavored Brandy
1¼ oz. Old Mr. Boston Dry Gin
1 Teaspoon Grenadine
Shake well with cracked ice and strain into 3 oz. cocktail glass.

FLIPS

See Index on page 143 for complete list of FLIP recipes.

FLORADORA COOLER

Into 12 oz. Tom Collins glass, put:
Juice 1 Lime
½ Teaspoon Powdered Sugar
½ oz. Raspberry Syrup or Grenadine
2 oz. Carbonated Water, and stir
Fill glass with cracked ice and add:
2 oz. Old Mr. Boston Dry Gin. *Fill with carbonated water or ginger ale and stir again.*

FLYING GRASSHOPPER COCKTAIL

¾ oz. Old Mr. Boston Creme de Menthe (green)
¾ oz. Old Mr. Boston Creme de Cacao (white)
¾ oz. Old Mr. Boston Vodka
Stir well with cracked ice and strain into 3 oz. cocktail glass.

FLYING SCOTCHMAN COCKTAIL

1 oz. Sweet Vermouth
1 oz. Old Mr. Boston Scotch Whisky
1 Dash Bitters
¼ Teaspoon Simple Syrup
Stir well with cracked ice and strain into 3 oz. cocktail glass.

FOG HORN

1 Cube of Ice
Juice of ½ Lime
1½ oz. Old Mr. Boston Dry Gin
Fill 8 oz. highball glass with ginger ale and stir. Leave lime in glass.

FOX RIVER COCKTAIL

½ oz. Old Mr. Boston Creme de Cacao
2 oz. Old Mr. Boston Whiskey*
4 Dashes Bitters
Stir well with cracked ice and strain into 3 oz. cocktail glass.

FRANKENJACK COCKTAIL

1 oz. Old Mr. Boston Dry Gin
¾ oz. Dry Vermouth
½ oz. Old Mr. Boston Apricot Flavored Brandy
1 Teaspoon Triple Sec
Stir well with cracked ice and strain into 3 oz. cocktail glass. Serve with cherry.

FRENCH "75"

Juice of 1 Lemon
2 Teaspoons Powdered Sugar
Stir well in 12 oz. Tom Collins glass. Then add 1 Cube of Ice, 2 oz. Old Mr. Boston Dry Gin and fill with Champagne and stir gently. Decorate with slice of lemon, orange and a cherry. Serve with straws.

*Bourbon, Blended, Rye or Canadian

FRISCO SOUR

Juice ¼ Lemon
Juice ½ Lime
½ oz. Benedictine
2 oz. Old Mr. Boston Whiskey*
Shake well with cracked ice and strain into 6 oz. sour glass. Fill with carbonated water and stir. Decorate with slices of lemon and lime.

FROTH BLOWER COCKTAIL

White of 1 Egg
1 Teaspoon Grenadine
2 oz. Old Mr. Boston Dry Gin
Shake well with cracked ice and strain into 4 oz. cocktail glass.

FROUPE COCKTAIL

1¼ oz. Sweet Vermouth
1¼ oz. Old Mr. Boston Five Star Brandy
1 Teaspoon Benedictine
Stir well with cracked ice and strain into 3 oz. cocktail glass.

FROZEN DAIQUIRI COCKTAIL

Juice 1 Lime
1 Teaspoon Powdered Sugar
2 oz. Old Mr. Boston Imported Rum
Agitate in electric mixer filled with shaved ice for about 2 minutes. Strain through coarse meshed strainer into 6 oz. Champagne glass.

GENERAL HARRISON'S EGGNOG

1 Egg
1 Teaspoon Powdered Sugar
Shake well with cracked ice and strain into 12 oz. Tom Collins glass. Fill glass with Claret or sweet cider and stir gently. Grate nutmeg on top.

GIBSON COCKTAIL

See *Special Martini Section* on pages 116 and 117.

* *Bourbon, Blended, Rye or Canadian.*

GILROY COCKTAIL

Juice of ¼ Lemon
½ oz. Dry Vermouth
¾ oz. Old Mr. Boston Wild Cherry Flavored Brandy
¾ oz. Old Mr. Boston Dry Gin
1 Dash Orange Bitters
Shake well with cracked ice and strain into 3 oz. cocktail glass.

39

GIMLET COCKTAIL

Juice 1 Lime
1 Teaspoon Powdered Sugar
1½ oz. Old Mr. Boston Dry Gin
Shake well with cracked ice and strain into 4 oz. cocktail glass; fill balance with carbonated water and stir.

GIN AND BITTERS

Put ½ teaspoon bitters into 3 oz. cocktail glass and revolve glass until it is entirely coated with the bitters. Then fill with Old Mr. Boston Dry Gin. *No ice is used in this drink.*

GIN AND IT (English)

2 oz. Old Mr. Boston Dry Gin
1 oz. Sweet Vermouth
Stir. No ice is used in this drink. Serve in 3 oz. cocktail glass.

GIN AND TONIC

2 oz. Old Mr. Boston Dry Gin
Cube of Ice
Fill glass with quinine water and stir. Use 12 oz. Tom Collins glass.

GIN BUCK

1 Cube of Ice
Juice of ½ Lemon
1½ oz. Old Mr. Boston Dry Gin
Fill 8 oz. highball glass with ginger ale and stir.

GIN COBBLER

Dissolve: 1 Teaspoon Powdered Sugar *in* 2 oz. Carbonated Water, *then fill* 10 oz. goblet with shaved ice, and add
2 oz. Old Mr. Boston Dry Gin
Stir well and decorate with fruits in season. Serve with straws.

GIN COCKTAIL

2 oz. Old Mr. Boston Dry Gin
2 Dashes Bitters
Stir well with cracked ice and strai.. into 3 oz. cocktail glass. Serve with . twist of lemon peel.

GIN COOLER

Into 12 oz. Tom Collins glass, put:
½ Teaspoon Powdered Sugar
2 oz. Carbonated Water, and stir
Fill glass with cracked ice and add.
2 oz. Old Mr. Boston Dry Gin
Fill with carbonated water or gin ger ale and stir again. Insert spir.. of orange or lemon peel (or both) an dangle end over rim of glass.

GIN DAISY

Juice of ½ Lemon
½ Teaspoon Powdered Sugar
1 Teaspoon Raspberry Syrup . Grenadine
2 oz. Old Mr. Boston Dry Gin
Shake well with cracked ice an strain into stein or 8 oz. metal cu.. Add cube of ice and decorate wi.. fruit.

GIN FIX

Juice ½ Lemon
1 Teaspoon Powdered Sugar
1 Teaspoon Water
Stir and fill glass with shaved i.. Add
2½ oz. Old Mr. Boston Dry Gin
Use 8 oz. highball glass. Stir we.. Add slice of lemon. Serve with stra..

G

GIN FIZZ

Juice ½ Lemon
1 Teaspoon Powdered Sugar
2 oz. Old Mr. Boston Dry Gin
Shake well with cracked ice and strain into 7 oz. highball glass. Fill with carbonated water and stir.

GIN HIGHBALL

1 Cube of Ice
2 oz. Old Mr. Boston Dry Gin
Fill 8 oz. highball glass with ginger ale or carbonated water. Add twist of lemon peel, if desired, and stir.

GIN MILK PUNCH

1 Teaspoon Powdered Sugar
2 oz. Old Mr. Boston Dry Gin
½ pt. Milk
Shake well with cracked ice, strain into 12 oz. Tom Collins glass and grate nutmeg on top.

GIN RICKEY

1 Cube of Ice
Juice ½ Lime
1½ oz. Old Mr. Boston Dry Gin
Fill 8 oz. highball glass with carbonated water and stir. Leave lime in glass.

GIN SANGAREE

Dissolve ½ teaspoon powdered sugar in 1 teaspoon of water. Add
2 oz. Old Mr. Boston Dry Gin
2 cubes of ice.
Serve in 8 oz. highball glass. Fill balance with soda water. Stir, leaving enough room on which to float a tablespoon of Port Wine. Sprinkle lightly with nutmeg.

GIN SLING

Dissolve 1 teaspoon powdered sugar in 1 teaspoon water and juice ½ lemon.
2 oz. Old Mr. Boston Dry Gin
2 Cubes of Ice
Serve in Old Fashioned cocktail glass and stir. Twist of orange peel and drop in glass.

GIN SMASH

Muddle 1 Lump of Sugar with
1 oz. Carbonated Water and
4 Sprigs of Green Mint
Add 2 oz. Old Mr. Boston Dry Gin and a cube of ice. Stir and decorate with a slice of orange and a cherry. Twist lemon peel on top. Use Old Fashioned cocktail glass.

GIN SOUR

Juice of ½ Lemon
½ Teaspoon Powdered Sugar
2 oz. Old Mr. Boston Dry Gin
Shake well with cracked ice and strain into 6 oz. sour glass. Fill with carbonated water and stir. Decorate with a half-slice of lemon and a cherry.

GIN SQUIRT

1½ oz. Old Mr. Boston Dry Gin
1 Tablespoon Powdered Sugar
1 Teaspoon Raspberry Syrup or Grenadine

Stir well with cracked ice and strain into 8 oz. highball glass; fill with carbonated water and stir. Decorate with cubes of pineapple and strawberries.

GIN SWIZZLE

Into 12 oz. Tom Collins glass put:
Juice 1 Lime
1 Teaspoon Powdered Sugar
2 oz. Carbonated Water
Fill glass with shaved ice and stir thoroughly with swizzle stick. Then add:
2 Dashes Bitters
2 oz. Old Mr. Boston Dry Gin
Fill with carbonated water and serve with swizzle stick in glass, allowing individual to do final stirring.

GIN TODDY

Use Old Fashioned cocktail glass.
½ Teaspoon Powdered Sugar
2 Teaspoons Water *and stir.*
2 oz. Old Mr. Boston Dry Gin
1 Lump of Ice
Stir well and twist lemon peel on top.

GIN TODDY (Hot)

Put lump of sugar into hot whiskey glass and fill two-thirds with boiling water. Add 2 oz. Old Mr. Boston Dry Gin. Stir and decorate with slice of lemon. Grate nutmeg on top.

GOLDEN FIZZ

Juice of ½ Lemon
1 Teaspoon Powdered Sugar
2 oz. Old Mr. Boston Dry Gin
Yolk of 1 Egg
Shake well with cracked ice and strain into 8 oz. highball glass. Fill with carbonated water and stir.

GOLDEN GATE COCKTAIL

1½ oz. Old Mr. Boston Dry Gin
1 Scoop Orange Sherbert
Shake well and strain into 4 oz. cocktail glass.

GOLDEN SLIPPER COCKTAIL

¾ oz. Yellow Chartreuse
2 oz. Old Mr. Boston Apricot Flavored Brandy
Stir well with cracked ice and strain into 4 oz. cocktail glass. Float yolk of egg on top.

GOLF COCKTAIL

1½ oz. Old Mr. Boston Dry Gin
¾ oz. Dry Vermouth
2 Dashes Bitters
Stir well with cracked ice and strain into 3 oz. cocktail glass.

Grand Royal Fizz

Juice ¼ Orange
Juice ½ Lemon
1 Teaspoon Powdered Sugar
2 oz. Old Mr. Boston Dry Gin
½ Teaspoon Maraschino
2 Teaspoons Sweet Cream
Shake well with cracked ice and strain into 8 oz. highball glass. Fill with carbonated water and stir.

Grapefruit Cocktail

1 oz. Grapefruit Juice
1 oz. Old Mr. Boston Dry Gin
1 Teaspoon Maraschino
Shake well with cracked ice and strain into 3 oz. cocktail glass. Serve with a cherry.

Grasshopper Cocktail

¾ oz. Old Mr. Boston Creme de Menthe (green)
¾ oz. Old Mr. Boston Creme de Cacao (white)
¾ oz. Light Sweet Cream
Shake well with cracked ice and strain into 3 oz. cocktail glass.

Green Dragon Cocktail

Juice of ¼ Lemon
½ oz. Old Mr. Boston Kummel
½ oz. Old Mr. Boston Creme de Menthe (Green)
1½ oz. Old Mr. Boston Dry Gin
4 Dashes Orange Bitters
Shake well with cracked ice and strain into 4 oz. cocktail glass.

Green Fizz

1 Teaspoon Powdered Sugar
White 1 Egg
Juice ½ Lemon
2 oz. Old Mr. Boston Dry Gin
1 Teaspoon Old Mr. Boston Creme de Menthe (Green)
Shake well with cracked ice and strain into 8 oz. highball glass. Fill with carbonated water and stir.

Green Swizzle

Make same as Gin Swizzle *(see page 43), and add 1 tablespoon Old Mr. Boston Green Creme de Menthe. If desired, rum, brandy or whiskey may be substituted for the gin.*

Grenadine Rickey

1 Cube of Ice
Juice ½ Lime
1½ oz. Grenadine
Fill 8 oz. highball glass with carbonated water and stir. Leave lime in glass.

Gypsy Cocktail

1¼ oz. Sweet Vermouth
1¼ oz. Old Mr. Boston Dry Gin
Stir well with cracked ice and strain into 3 oz. cocktail glass. Serve with a cherry.

HARLEM COCKTAIL

¾ oz. Pineapple Juice
1½ oz. Old Mr. Boston Dry Gin
½ Teaspoon Maraschino
2 Cubes of Pineapple
Shake well with cracked ice and strain into 3 oz. cocktail glass.

HARRY LAUDER COCKTAIL

1¼ oz. Old Mr. Boston Scotch
     Whisky
1¼ oz. Sweet Vermouth
½ Teaspoon Simple Syrup
Stir well with cracked ice and strain into 3 oz. cocktail glass.

HARVARD COCKTAIL

½ oz. Old Mr. Boston Five Star
     Brandy
¾ oz. Sweet Vermouth
Dash Bitters
1 Teaspoon Grenadine
2 Teaspoons Lemon Juice
Shake well with cracked ice and strain into 3 oz. cocktail glass.

HARVARD COOLER

Into 12 oz. Tom Collins glass put:
½ Teaspoon Powdered Sugar
2 oz. Carbonated Water
Stir. Then fill glass with cracked ice and add:
2 oz. Apple Brandy
Fill with carbonated water or ginger ale and stir again. Insert spiral of orange or lemon peel (or both) and dangle end over rim of glass.

HASTY COCKTAIL

¾ oz. Dry Vermouth
1½ oz. Old Mr. Boston Dry Gin
¼ Teaspoon Absinthe Substitute
1 Teaspoon Grenadine
Stir well with cracked ice and strain into 3 oz. cocktail glass.

HAVANA COCKTAIL

1¼ oz. Pineapple Juice
½ Teaspoon Lemon Juice
¾ oz. Old Mr. Boston Imported
     Rum
Shake well with cracked ice and strain into 3 oz. cocktail glass.

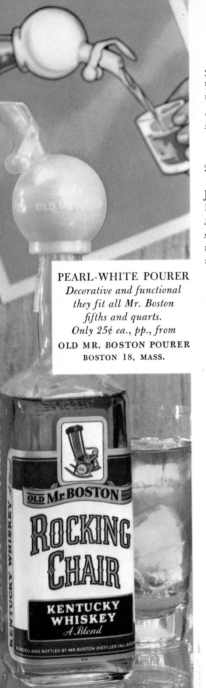

HAWAIIAN COCKTAIL

2 oz. Old Mr. Boston Dry Gin
½ oz. Pineapple Juice
½ oz. Curacao
*Shake well with cracked ice and
strain into 4 oz. cocktail glass.*

HI-DE-HO SPECIAL

2 oz. Old Mr. Boston Orange Flavored Gin
Juice of ½ Lemon
1 Teaspoon Powdered Sugar
*Shake well with cracked ice and
strain into 8 oz. highball glass. Fill
with seltzer water and stir. Decorate
with slice of lemon.*

HIGHBALLS

*See Index on page 144 for complete
list of* HIGHBALL *recipes.*

HIGHLAND COOLER

Into 12 oz. Tom Collins glass, put
½ Teaspoon Powdered Sugar
2 oz. Carbonated Water, *and stir.
Fill glass with cracked ice and add*
2 oz. Old Mr. Boston Scotch
Whisky
*Fill with carbonated water or gin-
ger ale and stir again. Insert spiral
of orange or lemon peel (or both) and
dangle end over rim of glass.*

HIGHLAND FLING COCKTAIL

¾ oz. Sweet Vermouth
1½ oz. Old Mr. Boston Scotch
Whisky
2 Dashes Orange Bitters
*Stir well with cracked ice and strain
into 3 oz. cocktail glass. Serve with
an olive.*

HOFFMAN HOUSE COCKTAIL

¾ oz. Dry Vermouth
1½ oz. Old Mr. Boston Dry Gin
2 Dashes Orange Bitters
Stir well with cracked ice and strain into 3 oz. cocktail glass. Serve with an olive.

HOLE-IN-ONE COCKTAIL

1½ oz. Old Mr. Boston Scotch Whisky
¾ oz. Dry Vermouth
¼ Teaspoon Lemon Juice
1 Dash Orange Bitters
Shake well with cracked ice and strain into 3 oz. cocktail glass.

HOLLYWOOD COOLER

Into 12 oz. Tom Collins glass, put:
2 oz. Frozen Orange Juice.
5 oz. California Sauterne Wine.
Ice cubes or shaved ice.
Sweeten as desired.
Stir well. Garnish with mint and half slice of orange.

HOMESTEAD COCKTAIL

1½ oz. Old Mr. Boston Dry Gin
¾ oz. Sweet Vermouth
Stir well with cracked ice and strain into 3 oz. cocktail glass and serve with slice of orange.

HONEYMOON COCKTAIL

¾ oz. Benedictine
¾ oz. Apple Brandy
Juice of ½ Lemon
1 Teaspoon Curacao
Shake well with cracked ice and strain into 3 oz. cocktail glass.

HONOLULU COCKTAIL No. 1

1 Dash Bitters
¼ Teaspoon Orange Juice
¼ Teaspoon Pineapple Juice
¼ Teaspoon Lemon Juice
½ Teaspoon Powdered Sugar
1½ oz. Old Mr. Boston Dry Gin
Shake well with cracked ice and strain into 3 oz. cocktail glass.

HONOLULU COCKTAIL No. 2

¾ oz. Old Mr. Boston Dry Gin
¾ oz. Maraschino
¾ oz. Benedictine
Stir well with cracked ice and strain into 3 oz. cocktail glass.

HOOT MON COCKTAIL

¾ oz. Sweet Vermouth
1½ oz. Old Mr. Boston Scotch Whisky
1 Teaspoon Benedictine
Stir well with cracked ice and strain into 3 oz. cocktail glass. Twist of lemon peel and drop in glass.

HOP TOAD COCKTAIL

Juice ½ Lime
¾ oz. Old Mr. Boston Apricot Flavored Brandy
¾ oz. Old Mr. Boston Imported Rum
Stir well with cracked ice and strain into 3 oz. cocktail glass.

HORSES NECK (With a Kick)

Peel rind of whole lemon in spiral fashion and put in 12 oz. Tom Collins glass with one end hanging over the rim. Fill glass with ice cubes. Add 2 oz. Old Mr. Boston Whiskey.* Then fill with ginger ale and stir well.

47

Bourbon, Blended, Rye or Canadian.

Hot Brandy Flip

1 Egg
1 Teaspoon Powdered Sugar
1½ oz. Old Mr. Boston Five Star Brandy
Beat egg, sugar and brandy and pour into Tom & Jerry Mug and fill with hot milk. Grate nutmeg on top.

Hot Brick Toddy

Into hot whiskey glass, put:
1 Teaspoon Butter
1 Teaspoon Powdered Sugar
3 Pinches Cinnamon
1 oz. Hot Water
Dissolve thoroughly. Then add:
1½ oz. Old Mr. Boston Whiskey*
Fill with boiling water and stir.

Hot Buttered Rum

Put lump of sugar into hot whiskey glass and fill two-thirds with boiling water. Add square of butter and 2 oz. Old Mr. Boston Imported Rum. Stir and grate nutmeg on top.

Hot Buttered Wine

For each serving—heat ½ cup Muscatel Wine. Add ¼ cup water just to simmering; do not boil. Preheat mug or cup with boiling water. Pour heated wine mixture into mug and add 1 teaspoon butter and 2 teaspoons maple syrup. Stir well and sprinkle nutmeg on top. Serve at once.

Hot Drinks

See Index on page 144 for complete list of Hot Drink Recipes.

Hot Springs Cocktail

1½ oz. Dry White Wine
½ oz. Pineapple Juice
½ Teaspoon Maraschino
1 Dash Orange Bitters
Shake well with cracked ice and strain into 3 oz. cocktail glass.

Hotel Plaza Cocktail

¾ oz. Sweet Vermouth
¾ oz. Dry Vermouth
¾ oz. Old Mr. Boston Dry Gin
Crush 1 Slice of Pineapple
Stir well with cracked ice and strain into 3 oz. cocktail glass.

H. P. W. Cocktail

¼ oz. Dry Vermouth
¼ oz. Sweet Vermouth
1½ oz. Old Mr. Boston Dry Gin
Stir well with cracked ice and strain into 3 oz. cocktail glass. Twist of orange peel and drop in glass.

Hula-Hula Cocktail

¾ oz. Orange Juice
1½ oz. Old Mr. Boston Dry Gin
¼ Teaspoon Powdered Sugar
Shake well with cracked ice and strain into 3 oz. cocktail glass.

Huntsman Cocktail

1½ oz. Old Mr. Boston Vodka
½ oz. Jamaica Rum
Juice of ½ Lime
Powdered sugar to taste
Shake well with cracked ice and strain into 3 oz. cocktail glass.

* *Bourbon, Blended, Rye or Canadian*

ICE CREAM FLIP

1 Egg
1 oz. Maraschino
1 oz. Curacao
1 Small Scoop Vanilla Ice Cream
Shake well with cracked ice and strain into 5 oz. flip glass. Grate a little nutmeg on top.

IDEAL COCKTAIL

1 oz. Dry Vermouth
1 oz. Old Mr. Boston Dry Gin
1 Teaspoon Maraschino
1 Teaspoon Grapefruit or Lemon Juice
Shake well with cracked ice and strain into 3 oz. cocktail glass. Serve with a cherry.

IMPERIAL COCKTAIL

¾ oz. Dry Vermouth
¾ oz. Old Mr. Boston Dry Gin
1 Teaspoon Maraschino
1 Dash Bitters
Stir well with cracked ice and strain into 3 oz. cocktail glass. Serve with a cherry.

IMPERIAL FIZZ

Juice of ½ Lemon
½ oz. Old Mr. Boston Imported Rum
1½ oz. Old Mr. Boston Whiskey*
1 Teaspoon Powdered Sugar
Shake well with cracked ice and strain into 7 oz. highball glass. Fill with carbonated water and stir.

INCOME TAX COCKTAIL

¼ oz. Dry Vermouth
¼ oz. Sweet Vermouth
1 oz. Old Mr. Boston Dry Gin
1 Dash Bitters
Juice of ¼ Orange
Shake well with cracked ice and strain into 3 oz. cocktail glass.

IRISH COFFEE

Into a pre-warmed 8 oz. stemmed glass (or coffee cup), pour 1½ oz. Irish Whiskey. Add 1 or 2 teaspoons sugar and fill to within ½ inch of top with strong, very hot black coffee. Stir to dissolve sugar. Float to brim with chilled whipped cream. Do not stir. Drink through floating cream.

49

*Bourbon, Blended, Rye or Canadian.

Irish Rickey

1 Cube of Ice
Juice of ½ Lime
1½ oz. Irish Whiskey
Fill 8 oz. highball glass with carbonated water and stir. Leave lime in glass.

Irish Shillelagh

Juice ½ Lemon
1 Teaspoon Powdered Sugar
1½ oz. Irish Whiskey
½ oz. Old Mr. Boston Sloe Gin
½ oz. Old Mr. Boston Imported Rum
2 Slices of Peach
Shake well with cracked ice and strain into 5 oz. punch glass. Decorate with fresh raspberries, strawberries and a cherry.

Irish Whiskey Cocktail

½ Teaspoon Curacao
½ Teaspoon Absinthe Substitute
¼ Teaspoon Maraschino
1 Dash Bitters
2 oz. Irish Whiskey
Stir well with cracked ice and strain into 3 oz. cocktail glass. Serve with an olive.

Irish Whiskey Highball

1 Cube of Ice
2 oz. Irish Whiskey
Fill 8 oz. highball glass with ginger ale or carbonated water. Add twist of lemon peel, if desired, and stir.

Jack-in-the-Box Cocktail

1 oz. Apple Brandy
1 oz. Pineapple Juice
Dash of Bitters
Shake well with cracked ice and strain into 3 oz. cocktail glass.

Jack Rose Cocktail

1½ oz. Apple Brandy
Juice ½ Lime
1 Teaspoon Grenadine
Shake well with cracked ice and strain into 3 oz. cocktail glass.

JAMAICA GLOW COCKTAIL

1 oz. Old Mr. Boston Dry Gin
½ oz. Claret
½ oz. Orange Juice
1 Teaspoon Jamaica Rum
Shake well with cracked ice and strain into 3 oz. cocktail glass.

JAMAICA GRANITO

Small scoop of either Lemon or
    Orange Sherbet
1½ oz. Old Mr. Boston Five Star
    Brandy
1 oz. Curacao
Use 12 oz. Tom Collins glass and fill balance with carbonated water and stir. Grate nutmeg on top.

JAPANESE FIZZ

Juice ½ Lemon
1 Teaspoon Powdered Sugar
1½ oz. Old Mr. Boston Whiskey*
½ oz. Port Wine
White 1 Egg
Shake well with cracked ice and strain into 8 oz. highball glass. Fill with carbonated water and stir. Serve with slice of pineapple.

JERSEY LIGHTNING COCKTAIL

1½ oz. Apple Brandy
½ oz. Sweet Vermouth
Juice 1 Lime
Shake well with cracked ice and strain into 3 oz. cocktail glass.

* Bourbon, Blended, Rye or Canadian.

J

JEWEL COCKTAIL

¾ oz. Green Chartreuse
¾ oz. Sweet Vermouth
¾ oz. Old Mr. Boston Dry Gin
1 Dash Orange Bitters
*Stir well with cracked ice and strain
into 3 oz. cocktail glass. Serve with a
cherry.*

JEYPLAK COCKTAIL

1½ oz. Old Mr. Boston Dry Gin
¾ oz. Sweet Vermouth
¼ Teaspoon Absinthe Substitute
*Stir well with cracked ice and strain
into 3 oz. cocktail glass. Serve with a
cherry.*

JOCKEY CLUB COCKTAIL

1 Dash Bitters
¼ Teaspoon Old Mr. Boston
   Creme de Cacao
Juice of ¼ Lemon
1½ oz. Old Mr. Boston Dry Gin
*Shake well with cracked ice and
strain into 3 oz. cocktail glass.*

JOHN COLLINS

Juice ½ Lemon
1 Teaspoon Powdered Sugar
2 oz. Holland Gin
*Shake well with cracked ice and
strain into 12 oz. Tom Collins glass.
Add several cubes of ice, fill with carbonated water and stir. Decorate
with slice of orange, lemon and a
cherry. Serve with straws.*

JOHNNIE COCKTAIL

¾ oz. Curacao
1½ oz. Old Mr. Boston Sloe Gin
1 Teaspoon Old Mr. Boston
   Anisette
*Stir well with cracked ice and strain
into 3 oz. cocktail glass.*

JOURNALIST COCKTAIL

¼ oz. Dry Vermouth
¼ oz. Sweet Vermouth
1½ oz. Old Mr. Boston Dry Gin
½ Teaspoon Lemon Juice
½ Teaspoon Curacao
1 Dash Bitters
*Shake well with cracked ice and
strain into 3 oz. cocktail glass.*

JUDGE JR. COCKTAIL

¾ oz. Old Mr. Boston Dry Gin
¾ oz. Old Mr. Boston Imported
   Rum
Juice of ¼ Lemon
½ Teaspoon Powdered Sugar
¼ Teaspoon Grenadine
*Shake well with cracked ice and
strain into 3 oz. cocktail glass.*

JUDGETTE COCKTAIL

¾ oz. Old Mr. Boston Peach
   Flavored Brandy
¾ oz. Old Mr. Boston Dry Gin
¾ oz. Dry Vermouth
Juice of ¼ Lime
*Shake well with cracked ice and
strain into 3 oz. cocktail glass. Serve
with a cherry.*

JULEPS

*See Index on page 144 for complete
list of* JULEP *recipes.*

K

Kangaroo Cocktail
1½ oz. Old Mr. Boston Vodka
¾ oz. Dry Vermouth
Stir well with cracked ice and strain into 3 oz. cocktail glass. Serve with twist of lemon peel.

K. C. B. Cocktail
½ oz. Old Mr. Boston Kummel
1½ oz. Old Mr. Boston Dry Gin
¼ Teaspoon Old Mr. Boston Apricot Flavored Brandy
¼ Teaspoon Lemon Juice
Shake well with cracked ice and strain into 3 oz. cocktail glass. Add twist of lemon peel and drop in glass.

Kentucky Cocktail
1½ oz. Pineapple Juice
¾ oz. Old Mr. Boston Kentucky Bourbon Whiskey
Shake well with cracked ice and strain into 3 oz. cocktail glass.

Kentucky Colonel Cocktail
½ oz. Benedictine
1½ oz. Old Mr. Boston Kentucky Bourbon Whiskey
Twist of Lemon Peel
Stir well with cracked ice and strain into a 3 oz. cocktail glass.

King Cole Cocktail
1 Slice of Orange
1 Slice of Pineapple
½ Teaspoon Powdered Sugar
Muddle well in Old Fashioned cocktail glass and add:
2 oz. Old Mr. Boston Whiskey*
1 Cube of Ice
Stir well.

53

* *Bourbon, Blended, Rye or Canadian.*

KISS-IN-THE-DARK COCKTAIL

¾ oz. Old Mr. Boston Dry Gin
¾ oz. Old Mr. Boston Wild Cherry
  Flavored Brandy
¾ oz. Dry Vermouth
*Stir well with cracked ice and strain
into 3 oz. cocktail glass.*

KLONDIKE COOLER

Into 12 oz. Tom Collins glass, put:
1 Teaspoon Powdered Sugar
2 oz. Carbonated Water
*Stir and fill glass with cracked ice
and add:*
2 oz. Old Mr. Boston Whiskey*
*Fill with carbonated water or gin-
ger ale and stir again. Insert spiral
of orange or lemon peel (or both) and
dangle end over rim of glass.*

KNICKERBOCKER COCKTAIL

1 Teaspoon Sweet Vermouth
1 oz. Dry Vermouth
1½ oz. Old Mr. Boston Dry Gin
*Stir well with cracked ice, strain into
3 oz. glass. Add twist of lemon peel
and drop in glass.*

KNICKERBOCKER SPECIAL COCKTAIL

1 Teaspoon Raspberry Syrup
1 Teaspoon Lemon Juice
1 Teaspoon Orange Juice
2 oz. Old Mr. Boston Imported
  Rum
½ Teaspoon Curacao
*Shake well with cracked ice and
strain into 4 oz. cocktail glass. Decorate with small slice of pineapple.*

KNOCK-OUT COCKTAIL

½ oz. Absinthe Substitute
¾ oz. Old Mr. Boston Dry Gin
¾ oz. Dry Vermouth
1 Teaspoon Old Mr. Boston
  Creme de Menthe (white)
*Stir well with cracked ice and strain
into 3 oz. cocktail glass. Serve with a
cherry.*

KRETCHMA COCKTAIL

1 oz. Old Mr. Boston Vodka
1 oz. Old Mr. Boston Creme de
  Cacao
½ oz. Lemon Juice
1 Dash Grenadine
*Shake well with cracked ice and
strain into 3 oz. cocktail glass.*

KUP'S INDISPENSABLE COCKTAIL

½ oz. Sweet Vermouth
½ oz. Dry Vermouth
1¼ oz. Old Mr. Boston Dry Gin
1 Dash Bitters
*Stir well with cracked ice and strain
into 3 oz. cocktail glass.*

Bourbon, Blended, Rye or Canadian.

Old Mr. Boston Distilled Dry Gin 80 and 90 Proof 100% Grain Neutral Spirits

L

LADIES' COCKTAIL
1¾ oz. Old Mr. Boston Whiskey*
½ Teaspoon Absinthe Substitute
½ Teaspoon Old Mr. Boston
    Anisette
2 Dashes Bitters
Stir well with cracked ice and strain into 3 oz. cocktail glass. Serve with a piece of pineapple on top.

LADY LOVE FIZZ
1 Teaspoon Powdered Sugar
Juice of ½ Lemon
White of 1 Egg
2 oz. Old Mr. Boston Dry Gin
2 Teaspoons Sweet Cream
Shake well with cracked ice and strain into 8 oz. highball glass. Fill with carbonated water and stir.

LASKY COCKTAIL
¾ oz. Grape Juice
¾ oz. Swedish Punch
¾ oz. Old Mr. Boston Dry Gin
Shake well with cracked ice and strain into 3 oz. cocktail glass.

LAWHILL COCKTAIL
¾ oz. Dry Vermouth
1½ oz. Old Mr. Boston Whiskey
¼ Teaspoon Absinthe Substitute
¼ Teaspoon Maraschino
1 Dash Bitters
Stir well with cracked ice and strain into 3 oz. cocktail glass.

LEAP FROG HIGHBALL
Juice ½ Lemon
2 oz. Old Mr. Boston Dry Gin
1 Cube of Ice
Fill 8 oz. highball glass with ginger ale and stir gently.

LEAP YEAR COCKTAIL
1¼ oz. Old Mr. Boston Dry Gin
½ oz. Old Mr. Boston Orange
    Flavored Gin
½ oz. Sweet Vermouth
¼ Teaspoon Lemon Juice
Shake well with cracked ice and strain into 3 oz. cocktail glass.

* *Bourbon, Blended, Rye or Canadian*

L

Leave It to Me Cocktail No. 1

oz. Old Mr. Boston Apricot Flavored Brandy
oz. Dry Vermouth
oz. Old Mr. Boston Dry Gin
Teaspoon Lemon Juice
Teaspoon Grenadine
hake well with cracked ice and rain into 3 oz. cocktail glass.

Leave It to Me Cocktail No. 2

Teaspoon Raspberry Syrup
Teaspoon Lemon Juice
Teaspoon Maraschino
2 oz. Old Mr. Boston Dry Gin
r well with cracked ice and strain to 3 oz. cocktail glass.

Lemon Squash

Lemon, peeled and quartered
Teaspoons Powdered Sugar
uddle well in 12 oz. Tom Collins ass until juice is well extracted. en fill glass with cracked ice. Add rbonated water and stir. Decorate th fruits.

Lemonade (Carbonated)

Teaspoons Powdered Sugar
ice 1 Lemon
r. Then fill 12 oz. Tom Collins ss with shaved ice. Add enough bonated water to fill glass and r. Decorate with slice of orange, non and a cherry. Serve with aws.

Lemonade (Claret)

2 Teaspoons Powdered Sugar
Juice 1 Lemon
Stir. Then fill 12 oz. Tom Collins glass with shaved ice. Add enough water to fill glass, leaving room to float 2 oz. Claret. Decorate with slice of orange, lemon and a cherry. Serve with straws.

Lemonade (Egg)

Juice 1 Lemon
2 Teaspoons Powdered Sugar
1 Whole Egg
Shake well and strain into 12 oz. Tom Collins glass filled with shaved ice. Add enough water to fill glass. Serve with straws.

Lemonade (Fruit)

Juice 1 Lemon
2 Teaspoons Powdered Sugar
1 oz. Raspberry Syrup
Stir. Then fill 12 oz. Tom Collins glass with shaved ice. Add enough water to fill glass and stir. Decorate with a slice of orange, lemon and a cherry. Serve with straws.

Lemonade (Golden)

Juice 1 Lemon
2 Teaspoons Powdered Sugar
Yolk of 1 Egg
6 oz. Water
Shake well with cracked ice and strain into 12 oz. Tom Collins glass. Decorate with a slice of orange, lemon and a cherry.

LEMONADE (Modern)

2 Teaspoons Powdered Sugar
1½ oz. Sherry Wine
1 oz. Old Mr. Boston Sloe Gin
Cut lemon in quarters and muddle well with sugar. Add sherry and sloe gin. Shake well with cracked ice and strain into 12 oz. Tom Collins glass. Fill glass with carbonated water.

LEMONADE (Plain)

2 Teaspoons Powdered Sugar
Juice 1 Lemon
Stir. Then fill 12 oz. Tom Collins glass with shaved ice. Add enough water to fill glass and stir well. Decorate with slice of orange, lemon and a cherry.

LIBERTY COCKTAIL

¾ oz. Old Mr. Boston Imported Rum
1½ oz. Apple Brandy
¼ Teaspoon Simple Syrup
Stir well with cracked ice and strain into 3 oz. cocktail glass.

LIMEADE

Juice 3 Limes
3 Teaspoons Powdered Sugar
Fill 12 oz. Tom Collins glass with shaved ice. Add enough water to fill glass. Stir well and drop lime in glass. Add a cherry. Serve with straws.

LINSTEAD COCKTAIL

1 oz. Old Mr. Boston Whiskey*
1 oz. Pineapple Juice
½ Teaspoon Powdered Sugar
¼ Teaspoon Absinthe Substitute
¼ Teaspoon Lemon Juice
Shake well with cracked ice and strain into 3 oz. cocktail glass.

LITTLE DEVIL COCKTAIL

Juice of ¼ Lemon
¼ oz. Triple Sec
¾ oz. Old Mr. Boston Imported Rum
¾ oz. Old Mr. Boston Dry Gin
Shake well with cracked ice and strain into 3 oz. cocktail glass.

LITTLE PRINCESS COCKTAIL

1¼ oz. Sweet Vermouth
1¼ oz. Old Mr. Boston Imported Rum
Stir well with cracked ice and strain into 3 oz. cocktail glass.

LONDON BUCK

1 Cube of Ice
2 oz. Old Mr. Boston Dry Gin
Juice of ½ Lemon
Fill 8 oz. highball glass with ginger ale and stir gently.

LONDON COCKTAIL

2 oz. Old Mr. Boston Dry Gin
2 Dashes Orange Bitters
½ Teaspoon Simple Syrup
½ Teaspoon Maraschino
Stir well with cracked ice and strain into 3 oz. cocktail glass. Add twist of lemon peel to glass.

LONDON SPECIAL COCKTAIL

Put rind of ½ orange into 6 oz. Champagne glass. Add:
1 Lump Sugar
2 Dashes Bitters
Fill with Champagne, well chilled, and stir gently.

---

* *Bourbon, Blended, Rye or Canadian.*

◄ Sloe Gin, Mint and Orange Flavored Gins 70 Proof

LONE TREE COCKTAIL

¾ oz. Sweet Vermouth
1½ oz. Old Mr. Boston Dry Gin
Stir well with cracked ice and strain into 3 oz. cocktail glass.

LONE TREE COOLER

Into 12 oz. Tom Collins glass, put:
½ Teaspoon Powdered Sugar
2 oz. Carbonated Water
Stir and fill glass with cracked ice and add:
2 oz. Old Mr. Boston Dry Gin
½ oz. Dry Vermouth
Fill with carbonated water or ginger ale and stir again. Insert spiral of orange or lemon peel (or both) and dangle end over rim of glass.

LOS ANGELES COCKTAIL

Juice of ½ Lemon
1 Teaspoon Powdered Sugar
1 Egg
¼ Teaspoon Sweet Vermouth
1½ oz. Old Mr. Boston Whiskey*
Shake well with cracked ice and strain into 4 oz. cocktail glass.

LOVE COCKTAIL

2 oz. Old Mr. Boston Sloe Gin
White of 1 Egg
½ Teaspoon Lemon Juice
½ Teaspoon Raspberry Juice
Shake well with cracked ice and strain into 4 oz. cocktail glass.

LOVING CUP

Use large Glass Pitcher.
4 Teaspoons Powdered Sugar
6 oz. Carbonated Water
1 oz. Triple Sec
2 oz. Old Mr. Boston Five Star Brandy
Fill pitcher with cubes of ice. Add 1 pint Claret. Stir well and decorate with as many fruits as available and also rind of cucumber inserted on each side of pitcher. Top with small bunch of mint sprigs.

LUXURY COCKTAIL

3 oz. Old Mr. Boston Five Star Brandy
2 Dashes Orange Bitters
3 oz. well chilled Champagne
Stir very gently. Use 6 oz. Saucer Champagne glass.

* *Bourbon, Blended, Rye or Canadian*

M

MAIDEN'S BLUSH COCKTAIL

¼ Teaspoon Lemon Juice
1 Teaspoon Curacao
1 Teaspoon Grenadine
1½ oz. Old Mr. Boston Dry Gin
Shake well with cracked ice and strain into 3 oz. cocktail glass.

MAI-TAI

½ Teaspoon Powdered Sugar
2 oz. Old Mr. Boston Imported
    Rum
1 oz. Curacao
½ oz. Orgeat or any almond
    flavored syrup
½ oz. Grenadine
½ oz. Fresh Lime Juice
Shake well with cracked ice and strain into large Old Fashioned cocktail glass about ⅓ full with crushed ice. Decorate with Maraschino cherry speared to wedge of preferably fresh pineapple. For a fair raiser top with a dash of 151 proof rum and for a real Hawaiian effect float an orchid on each drink.

MAJOR BAILEY

¼ oz. Lime Juice
¼ oz. Lemon Juice
½ Teaspoon Powdered Sugar
12 Mint Leaves
Muddle well and pour into 12 oz. Tom Collins glass filled with shaved ice, and add: 2 oz. Old Mr. Boston Dry Gin. *Stir gently, until glass is frosted. Decorate with spring of mint and serve with straws.*

MAMIE GILROY

Juice ½ Lime
2 Cubes of Ice
2 oz. Old Mr. Boston Scotch
    Whisky
1 Dash Bitters
Fill 12 oz. Tom Collins glass with carbonated water and stir gently.

MAMIE TAYLOR

Juice ½ Lime
2 Cubes of Ice
2 oz. Old Mr. Boston Scotch
    Whisky
Fill 12 oz. Tom Collins glass with ginger ale and stir gently.

61

MAMIE'S SISTER

Juice 1 Lime
Drop rind in glass.
2 Cubes of Ice
2 oz. Old Mr. Boston Dry Gin
Fill 12 oz. Tom Collins glass with ginger ale and stir gently.

MANHATTAN COCKTAIL

1 Dash Bitters
¾ oz. Sweet Vermouth
1½ oz. Old Mr. Boston Whiskey*
Stir well with cracked ice and strain into 3 oz. cocktail glass. Serve with a cherry.

MANHATTAN COCKTAIL (Dry)

1 Dash Bitters
¾ oz. Dry Vermouth
1½ oz. Old Mr. Boston Whiskey*
Stir well with cracked ice and strain into 3 oz. cocktail glass. Serve with an olive.

MANHATTAN COCKTAIL (Sweet)

1 Dash Bitters
¾ oz. Sweet Vermouth
1½ oz. Old Mr. Boston Whiskey*
Stir well with cracked ice and strain into 3 oz. cocktail glass. Serve with a cherry.

MANILA FIZZ

2 oz. Old Mr. Boston Dry Gin
1 Egg
1 Teaspoon Powdered Sugar
2 oz. Sarsaparilla
Juice of 1 Lime or ½ Lemon
Shake well with cracked ice and strain into 10 oz. Pilsner glass.

MARGARITA COCKTAIL

1½ oz. Tequila
½ oz. Triple Sec
Juice of ½ Lemon or Lime
Stir with crushed ice. Rub rim of 3 oz. cocktail glass with rind of lemon or lime, dip rim in salt, pour and serve.

MARTINEZ COCKTAIL

1 Dash Orange Bitters
1 oz. Dry Vermouth
¼ Teaspoon Curacao
1 oz. Old Mr. Boston Dry Gin
Stir well with cracked ice and strain into 3 oz. cocktail glass. Serve with a cherry.

MARTINI COCKTAIL

See *Special Martini Section* on pages 116 and 117.

MARY GARDEN COCKTAIL

1½ oz. Dubonnet
¾ oz. Dry Vermouth
Stir well with cracked ice and strain into 3 oz. cocktail glass.

MARY PICKFORD COCKTAIL

1 oz. Old Mr. Boston Imported Rum
1 oz. Pineapple Juice
¼ Teaspoon Grenadine
¼ Teaspoon Maraschino
Shake well with cracked ice and strain into 3 oz. cocktail glass.

* *Bourbon, Blended, Rye or Canadian*

MAURICE COCKTAIL

Juice of ¼ Orange
½ oz. Sweet Vermouth
½ oz. Dry Vermouth
oz. Old Mr. Boston Dry Gin
Dash Bitters
Shake well with cracked ice and strain into 4 oz. cocktail glass.

MAY BLOSSOM FIZZ

Teaspoon Grenadine
Juice ½ Lemon
oz. Swedish Punch
Shake well with cracked ice and strain into 7 oz. highball glass. Fill with carbonated water and stir.

McCLELLAND COCKTAIL

oz. Curacao
½ oz. Old Mr. Boston Sloe Gin
Dash Orange Bitters
Shake well with cracked ice and strain into 3 oz. cocktail glass.

MELON COCKTAIL

oz. Old Mr. Boston Dry Gin
Teaspoon Lemon Juice
Teaspoon Maraschino
Shake well with cracked ice and strain into 3 oz. cocktail glass. Serve with a cherry.

MERRY WIDOW COCKTAIL No. 1

¼ oz. Old Mr. Boston Dry Gin
¾ oz. Dry Vermouth
Teaspoon Benedictine
Teaspoon Absinthe Substitute
Dash Orange Bitters
Stir well with cracked ice and strain into 3 oz. cocktail glass. Add twist of lemon peel and drop in glass.

MERRY WIDOW COCKTAIL No. 2

1¼ oz. Maraschino
1¼ oz. Old Mr. Boston Wild Cherry Flavored Brandy
Stir well with cracked ice and strain into 3 oz. cocktail glass. Serve with a cherry.

MERRY WIDOW FIZZ

Juice ½ Orange
Juice ½ Lemon
White of 1 Egg
1 Teaspoon Powdered Sugar
1½ oz. Old Mr. Boston Sloe Gin
Shake well with cracked ice and strain into 8 oz. highball glass. Fill with carbonated water and stir.

METROPOLITAN COCKTAIL

1¼ oz. Old Mr. Boston Five Star Brandy
1¼ oz. Sweet Vermouth
½ Teaspoon Simple Syrup
1 Dash Bitters
Stir well with cracked ice and strain into 3 oz. cocktail glass.

MEXICOLA

2 oz. Tequila
Juice ½ Lime
Use 12 oz. Tom Collins glass with cubes of ice. Fill balance with cola and stir gently.

MIAMI BEACH COCKTAIL

¾ oz. Old Mr. Boston Scotch
Whisky
¾ oz. Dry Vermouth
¾ oz. Grapefruit Juice
*Stir well with cracked ice and strain
into 3 oz. cocktail glass.*

MIDNIGHT COCKTAIL

1 oz. Old Mr. Boston Apricot
Flavored Brandy
½ oz. Curacao
½ oz. Lemon Juice
*Shake well with cracked ice and
strain into 3 oz. cocktail glass.*

MIKADO COCKTAIL

2 oz. Old Mr. Boston Five Star
Brandy
2 Dashes Bitters
½ Teaspoon Old Mr. Boston
Creme de Cacao
½ Teaspoon Curacao
*Shake well with cracked ice and
strain into 3 oz. cocktail glass.*

MILK PUNCH

1 Teaspoon Powdered Sugar
2 oz. Old Mr. Boston Whiskey*
½ pt. Milk
*Shake well with cracked ice and
strain into 12 oz. Tom Collins glass.
Grate nutmeg on top.*

MILLION DOLLAR COCKTAIL

2 Teaspoons Pineapple Juice
1 Teaspoon Grenadine
White of 1 Egg
¾ oz. Sweet Vermouth
1½ oz. Old Mr. Boston Dry Gin
*Shake well with cracked ice and
strain into 4 oz. cocktail glass.*

MILLIONAIRE COCKTAIL

White of 1 Egg
¼ Teaspoon Grenadine
½ oz. Curacao
1½ oz. Old Mr. Boston Whiskey
*Shake well with cracked ice and
strain into 4 oz. cocktail glass.*

MINNEHAHA COCKTAIL

Juice of ¼ Orange
½ oz. Dry Vermouth
½ oz. Sweet Vermouth
1 oz. Old Mr. Boston Dry Gin
*Shake well with cracked ice and
strain into 4 oz. cocktail glass.*

MINT COLLINS

Juice ½ Lemon
2 oz. Old Mr. Boston Mint Fl
vored Gin
*Shake well with cracked ice an
strain into 12 oz. Tom Collins gla
Add several cubes of ice, fill with ca
bonated water and stir. Decora
with slice of lemon, orange and
cherry. Serve with straws.*

MINT HIGHBALL

1 Cube of Ice
2 oz. Old Mr. Boston Creme
Menthe (green)
*Fill 8 oz. highball glass with ging
ale or carbonated water. Add tw
of lemon peel, if desired, and stir.*

* Bourbon, Blended, Rye or Canadi

MINT JULEP

to Silver Mug or 12 oz. Tom Collins glass put:

Sprigs of Mint
Teaspoon Powdered Sugar
Teaspoons of Water, and muddle
ill glass or mug with shaved ice,
ld 2½ oz. Old Mr. Boston Kentucky Straight Bourbon Whiskey,
id stir gently until glass is frosted.
ecorate with slice of orange, lemon,
ineapple and a cherry Insert 5 or
sprigs of mint on top. Serve with
raws.

MINT JULEP (Southern Style)

ill silver mug or 12 oz. Tom Collins
ass with finely shaved ice. Add 2½
. Old Mr. Boston Kentucky
raight Bourbon Whiskey *and stir
ntil glass is heavily frosted. (Do
ot hold glass with hand while stir-
ng.) Add 1 teaspoon powdered
gar and fill balance with water,
id stir. Decorate with 5 or 6 sprigs
' fresh mint so that the tops are
bout 2 inches above rim of mug or
ass. Use short straws so that it is
ecessary to bury nose in mint. The
int is intended for odor rather than
ste.*

MINT ON ROCKS

ur 2 oz. Old Mr. Boston Creme
Menthe (green) *on ice cubes in
d Fashioned cocktail glass.*

MR. MANHATTAN COCKTAIL

Muddle lump of sugar and
4 Sprigs of Mint
¼ Teaspoon Lemon Juice
1 Teaspoon Orange Juice
1½ oz. Old Mr. Boston Dry Gin
*Shake well with cracked ice and
strain into 3 oz. cocktail glass.*

MODERN COCKTAIL

1½ oz. Old Mr. Boston Scotch
   Whisky
½ Teaspoon Lemon Juice
¼ Teaspoon Absinthe Substitute
½ Teaspoon Jamaica Rum
1 Dash Orange Bitters
*Shake well with cracked ice and
strain into 3 oz. cocktail glass. Serve
with a cherry.*

MONTE CARLO IMPERIAL HIGHBALL

2 oz. Old Mr. Boston Dry Gin
½ oz. Old Mr. Boston Creme de
   Menthe (white)
Juice ¼ Lemon
*Shake well with cracked ice and
strain into 8 oz. highball glass. Fill
glass with Champagne and stir.*

MONTMARTRE COCKTAIL

1¼ oz. Old Mr. Boston Dry Gin
½ oz. Sweet Vermouth
½ oz. Triple Sec
*Stir well with cracked ice and strain
into 3 oz. cocktail glass. Serve with a
cherry.*

MORNING COCKTAIL

1 oz. Old Mr. Boston Five Star
    Brandy
1 oz. Dry Vermouth
¼ Teaspoon Curacao
¼ Teaspoon Maraschino
¼ Teaspoon Absinthe Substitute
2 Dashes Orange Bitters
*Stir well with cracked ice and strain
into 3 oz. cocktail glass. Serve with a
cherry.*

MORNING GLORY FIZZ

Juice ½ Lemon or 1 Lime
1 Teaspoon Powdered Sugar
White of 1 Egg
½ Teaspoon Absinthe Substitute
2 oz. Old Mr. Boston Scotch
    Whisky
*Shake well with cracked ice and
strain into 8 oz. highball glass. Fill
with carbonated water and stir.*

MOSCOW MULE

Into a Copper Mug, put:
1½ oz. Old Mr. Boston Vodka
Juice of ½ Lime
*Add ice cubes and fill with ginger
beer. Drop lime in mug to decorate.*

MOULIN ROUGE COCKTAIL

1½ oz. Old Mr. Boston Sloe Gin
¾ oz. Sweet Vermouth
1 Dash Bitters
*Stir well with cracked ice and stra
into 3 oz. cocktail glass.*

MOUNTAIN COCKTAIL

White of 1 Egg
¼ Teaspoon Lemon Juice
¼ Teaspoon Dry Vermouth
¼ Teaspoon Sweet Vermouth
1½ oz. Old Mr. Boston Whiske
*Shake well with cracked ice a
strain into 4 oz. cocktail glass.*

MULLED CLARET

Into a metal mug put:
1 Lump Sugar
Juice ½ Lemon
1 Dash Bitters
1 Teaspoon Mixed Cinnamon a
    Nutmeg
5 oz. Claret
*Heat poker red hot and hold in liq
until boiling and serve.*

* *Bourbon, Blended, Rye or Canad*

Napoleon Cocktail

oz. Old Mr. Boston Dry Gin
½ Teaspoon Curacao
½ Teaspoon Dubonnet
*Stir well with cracked ice and strain
into 3 oz. cocktail glass.*

Negronis

¾ oz. Old Mr. Boston Dry Gin
¾ oz. Campari Bitters
¾ oz. Sweet or Dry Vermouth
¾ oz. Soda Water
*Pour over ice cubes in Old Fashioned
cocktail glass and stir lightly.*

Nevada Cocktail

1½ oz. Old Mr. Boston Imported
   Rum
1 oz. Grapefruit Juice
Juice of 1 Lime
1 Dash Bitters
3 Teaspoons Powdered Sugar
*Shake well with cracked ice and
strain into 4 oz. cocktail glass.*

New Orleans Gin Fizz

Juice ½ Lemon
1 Teaspoon Powdered Sugar
White of 1 Egg
2 oz. Old Mr. Boston Dry Gin
1 Tablespoon Sweet Cream
½ Teaspoon Orange Flower Water
*Shake well with cracked ice and
strain into 12 oz. Tom Collins glass.
Fill with carbonated water and stir.*

New York Cocktail

Juice 1 Lime or ½ Lemon
1 Teaspoon Powdered Sugar
1½ oz. Old Mr. Boston Whiskey*
½ Teaspoon Grenadine
Twist of Orange Peel
*Shake well with cracked ice and
strain into 3 oz. cocktail glass. Add
twist of lemon peel and drop in glass.*

New York Sour

Juice ½ Lemon
1 Teaspoon Powdered Sugar
2 oz. Old Mr. Boston Whiskey*
*Shake well with cracked ice and
strain into 6 oz. sour glass, leaving
about ½ inch on which to float claret.
Decorate with a half-slice of lemon
and a cherry.*

* *Bourbon, Blended, Rye or Canadian.*

O

Night Cap

2 oz. Old Mr. Boston Imported
 Rum
1 Teaspoon Powdered Sugar
*Add enough warm milk to fill a Tom
& Jerry Mug and stir. Grate a little
nutmeg on top.*

North Pole Cocktail

White of 1 Egg
½ oz. Lemon Juice
½ oz. Maraschino
1 oz. Old Mr. Boston Dry Gin
*Shake well with cracked ice and
strain into 4 oz. cocktail glass and
top with whipped cream.*

Ninitchka Cocktail

1½ oz. Old Mr. Boston Vodka
½ oz. Old Mr. Boston Creme de
 Cacao
½ oz. Lemon Juice
*Shake well with cracked ice and
strain into 3 oz. cocktail glass.*

Old Fashioned Cocktail

Use Old Fashioned cocktail glass.
½ Lump of Sugar
2 Dashes Bitters
*Add enough water to cover sugar
and muddle well.*
1 Cube of Ice
2 oz. Old Mr. Boston Whiskey*
*Stir well. Add twist of lemon rind
and drop in glass. Decorate with
slice of orange, lemon and a cherry.
Serve with stirring rod.*

Old Pal Cocktail

½ oz. Grenadine
½ oz. Sweet Vermouth
1¼ oz. Old Mr. Boston Whiskey*
*Stir well with cracked ice and strain
into 3 oz. cocktail glass.*

* *Bourbon, Blended, Rye or Canadian*

O

OLYMPIC COCKTAIL

¾ oz. Orange Juice
¾ oz. Curacao
¾ oz. Old Mr. Boston Five Star Brandy
Shake well with cracked ice and strain into 3 oz. cocktail glass.

OPAL COCKTAIL

1 oz. Old Mr. Boston Dry Gin
½ oz. Orange Juice
½ oz. Triple Sec
¼ Teaspoon Powdered Sugar
½ Teaspoon Orange Flower Water
Shake well with cracked ice and strain into 3 oz. cocktail glass.

OPENING COCKTAIL

½ oz. Grenadine
½ oz. Sweet Vermouth
¾ oz. Old Mr. Boston Whiskey*
Stir well with cracked ice and strain into 3 oz. cocktail glass.

OPERA COCKTAIL

½ oz. Maraschino
½ oz. Dubonnet
1½ oz. Old Mr. Boston Dry Gin
Stir well with cracked ice and strain into 3 oz. cocktail glass.

ORANGEADE

Juice 2 Oranges
1 Teaspoon Powdered Sugar
Add 2 cubes of ice and enough water to fill 12 oz. Tom Collins glass and stir well. Decorate with a slice of orange, lemon and 2 cherries. Serve with straws.

ORANGE BLOSSOM COCKTAIL

1 oz. Old Mr. Boston Dry Gin
1 oz. Orange Juice
¼ Teaspoon Powdered Sugar
Shake well with cracked ice and strain into 3 oz. cocktail glass.

ORANGE GIN COLLINS

Juice ½ Lemon
2 oz. Old Mr. Boston Orange Flavored Gin
Shake well with cracked ice and strain into 12 oz. Tom Collins glass. Add several cubes of ice, fill with carbonated water and stir. Decorate with slice of lemon, orange and a cherry. Serve with straws.

ORANGE GIN FIZZ

Juice ½ Lemon
1 Teaspoon Powdered Sugar
2 oz. Old Mr. Boston Orange Flavored Gin
Shake well with cracked ice and strain into 7 oz. highball glass. Fill with carbonated water and stir.

ORANGE GIN HIGHBALL

1 Cube of Ice
2 oz. Old Mr. Boston Orange Flavored Gin
Fill 8 oz. highball glass with ginger ale or carbonated water. Add twist of lemon peel, if desired, and stir.

69

*Bourbon, Blended, Rye or Canadian.

Orange Gin Rickey

1 Cube of Ice
Juice ½ Lime
2 oz. Old Mr. Boston Orange Flavored Gin
Fill 8 oz. highball glass with carbonated water and stir. Leave lime in glass.

Orange Milk Fizz

Juice ½ Lemon
1 Teaspoon Powdered Sugar
2 oz. Old Mr. Boston Orange Flavored Gin
2 oz. Milk
Shake well with cracked ice and strain into 8 oz. highball glass. Fill with carbonated water and stir.

Orange Smile

1 Egg
Juice 1 Large Orange
1 Tablespoon Raspberry Syrup or Grenadine
Shake well with cracked ice and strain into 8 oz. stem goblet.

Orchid Cocktail

2 oz. Old Mr. Boston Dry Gin
1 Egg White
1 Dash of Creme de Yvette
Shake well with cracked ice and strain into 4 oz. cocktail glass.

Oriental Cocktail

1 oz. Old Mr. Boston Whiskey*
½ oz. Sweet Vermouth
½ oz. Curacao
Juice of ½ Lime
Shake well with cracked ice and strain into 3 oz. cocktail glass.

Paddy Cocktail

1¼ oz. Irish Whiskey
¾ oz. Sweet Vermouth
1 Dash Bitters
Stir well with cracked ice and strain into 3 oz. cocktail glass.

Palm Beach Cocktail

1½ oz. Old Mr. Boston Dry Gin
¼ oz. Sweet Vermouth
¼ oz. Grapefruit Juice
Shake well with cracked ice and strain into 3 oz. cocktail glass.

*Bourbon, Blended, Rye or Canadian.

PALMER COCKTAIL

2 oz. Old Mr. Boston Whiskey*
1 Dash Bitters
½ Teaspoon Lemon Juice
Stir well with cracked ice and strain into 3 oz. cocktail glass.

PALMETTO COCKTAIL

1¼ oz. Old Mr. Boston Imported
    Rum
1¼ oz. Dry Vermouth
2 Dashes Bitters
Stir well with cracked ice and strain into 3 oz. cocktail glass.

PANAMA COCKTAIL

1 oz. Old Mr. Boston Creme de
    Cacao
1 oz. Sweet Cream
1 oz. Old Mr. Boston Five Star
    Brandy
Shake well with cracked ice and strain into 4 oz. cocktail glass.

PARADISE COCKTAIL

1 oz. Old Mr. Boston Apricot Fla-
    vored Brandy
¾ oz. Old Mr. Boston Dry Gin
Juice ¼ Orange
Shake well with cracked ice and strain into 3 oz. cocktail glass.

PARISIAN BLONDE COCKTAIL

¾ oz. Sweet Cream
¾ oz. Curacao
¾ oz. Jamaica Rum
Shake well with cracked ice and strain into 3 oz. cocktail glass.

PASSION DAIQUIRI COCKTAIL

1½ oz. Old Mr. Boston Imported
    Rum
Juice 1 Lime
1 Teaspoon Powdered Sugar
½ oz. Passion Fruit Juice
Shake well with cracked ice and strain into 3 oz. cocktail glass.

PEACH BLOSSOM

1 Teaspoon Lemon Juice
½ Teaspoon Powdered Sugar
2 oz. Old Mr. Boston Dry Gin
½ Peach
Shake well with cracked ice and strain into 8 oz. highball glass. Fill with carbonated water and stir.

PEACH BLOW FIZZ

Juice ½ Lemon
White of 1 Egg
2 Teaspoons Grenadine
½ Teaspoon Powdered Sugar
1 oz. Sweet Cream
2 oz. Old Mr. Boston Dry Gin
Shake well with cracked ice an strain into 10 oz. highball glass. Fi with carbonated water and stir.

PEACH SANGAREE

2 oz. Old Mr. Boston Peach Fla
    vored Brandy
2 cubes of Ice
Serve in 8 oz. highball glass. F balance with soda water. Stir, leav ing enough room on which to float tablespoon of Port Wine. Sprink lightly with nutmeg.

* *Bourbon, Blended, Rye or Canadia*

PEGGY COCKTAIL

¾ oz. Dry Vermouth
1½ oz. Old Mr. Boston Dry Gin
¼ Teaspoon Absinthe Substitute
¼ Teaspoon Dubonnet
Stir well with cracked ice and strain into 3 oz. cocktail glass.

PENDENNIS TODDY

Muddle lump of sugar with 1 teaspoon of water, in 6 oz. sour glass. Fill with finely shaved ice, add 2 oz. Old Mr. Boston Whiskey* and stir. Decorate with 2 slices of lemon.

PERFECT COCKTAIL

¼ oz. Dry Vermouth
¼ oz. Sweet Vermouth
1½ oz. Old Mr. Boston Dry Gin
1 Dash Bitters
Stir well with cracked ice and strain into 3 oz. cocktail glass.

PETER PAN COCKTAIL

2 Dashes Bitters
¾ oz. Orange Juice
¾ oz. Dry Vermouth
¾ oz. Old Mr. Boston Dry Gin
Shake well with cracked ice and strain into 3 oz. cocktail glass.

PHOEBE SNOW COCKTAIL

1¼ oz. Dubonnet
1¼ oz. Old Mr. Boston Five Star Brandy
¼ Teaspoon Absinthe Substitute
Stir well with cracked ice and strain into 3 oz. cocktail glass.

PICCADILLY COCKTAIL

¾ oz. Dry Vermouth
1½ oz. Old Mr. Boston Dry Gin
¼ Teaspoon Absinthe Substitute
¼ Teaspoon Grenadine
Stir well with cracked ice and strain into 3 oz. cocktail glass.

PICON COCKTAIL

See AMER PICON COCKTAIL *on page 3.*

PIKE'S PEAK COOLER

Juice ½ Lemon
1 Teaspoon Powdered Sugar
1 Egg
Shake well with cracked ice and strain into 12 oz. Tom Collins glass and fill with hard cider and stir. Insert spiral of orange or lemon peel (or both) and dangle end over rim of glass.

PINEAPPLE COCKTAIL

¾ oz. Pineapple Juice
1½ oz. Old Mr. Boston Imported Rum
½ Teaspoon Lemon Juice
Shake well with cracked ice and strain into 3 oz. cocktail glass.

PINEAPPLE COOLER

Into 12 oz. Tom Collins glass, put:
½ Teaspoon Powdered Sugar
2 oz. Carbonated Water
Stir; fill glass with cracked ice and add: 2 oz. Dry White Wine. Fill with carbonated water and stir again. Insert spiral of orange or lemon peel (or both) and dangle end over rim of glass.

Bourbon, Blended, Rye or Canadian.

PINEAPPLE DREAM COCKTAIL

½ oz. Pineapple Juice
Juice of ½ Lime
1 oz. Old Mr. Boston Imported Rum
Shake well with cracked ice and strain into 3 oz. cocktail glass.

PINEAPPLE FIZZ

1 oz. Pineapple Juice
½ Teaspoon Powdered Sugar
2 oz. Old Mr. Boston Imported Rum
Shake well with cracked ice and strain into 7 oz. highball glass. Fill with carbonated water and stir.

PING-PONG COCKTAIL

Juice of ¼ Lemon
White of 1 Egg
1 oz. Old Mr. Boston Sloe Gin
1 oz. Creme de Yvette
Shake well with cracked ice and strain into 4 oz. cocktail glass.

PINK GIN

See GIN AND BITTERS *page 40.*

PINK LADY COCKTAIL

White of 1 Egg
1 Teaspoon Grenadine
1 Teaspoon Sweet Cream
1½ oz. Old Mr. Boston Dry Gin
Shake well with cracked ice and strain into 4 oz. cocktail glass.

PINK ROSE FIZZ

Juice ½ Lemon
1 Teaspoon Powdered Sugar
White of 1 Egg
½ Teaspoon Grenadine
2 Teaspoons Sweet Cream
2 oz. Old Mr. Boston Dry Gin
Shake well with cracked ice and strain into 8 oz. highball glass. Fill with carbonated water and stir.

PINK WHISKERS COCKTAIL

¾ oz. Old Mr. Boston Apricot Flavored Brandy
¾ oz. Dry Vermouth
1 oz. Orange Juice
1 Teaspoon Grenadine
¼ Teaspoon Old Mr. Boston Creme de Menthe (white)
Shake well with cracked ice and strain into 4 oz. cocktail glass and top with a little Port Wine.

PLAIN VERMOUTH COCKTAIL

See VERMOUTH COCKTAIL *page 103*

PLANTER'S COCKTAIL

Juice of ¼ Lemon
½ Teaspoon Powdered Sugar
1½ oz. Jamaica Rum
Shake well with cracked ice and strain into 3 oz. cocktail glass.

PLANTER'S PUNCH No. 1

Juice 2 Limes
2 Teaspoons Powdered Sugar
2 oz. Carbonated Water
*Fill 12 oz. Tom Collins glass with
shaved ice and stir until glass is
frosted. Add 2 dashes Bitters, 2½ oz.*
Old Mr. Boston Imported Rum.
*Stir and decorate with slice of lemon,
orange, pineapple and a cherry.
Serve with straws.*

PLANTER'S PUNCH No. 2

Juice 1 Lime
Juice ½ Lemon
Juice ½ Orange
1 Teaspoon Pineapple Juice
2 oz. Old Mr. Boston Imported
    Rum
*Pour above into 16 oz. glass, well
filled with shaved ice. Stir until glass
is frosted. Then add 1 oz. Jamaica
Rum, and top with ¼ teaspoon
Curacao. Decorate with slice of orange, lemon, pineapple and a cherry,
also sprig of mint dipped in powdered sugar. Serve with straws.*

PLAZA COCKTAIL

¾ oz. Sweet Vermouth
¾ oz. Dry Vermouth
¾ oz. Old Mr. Boston Dry Gin
1 Strip of Pineapple
*Shake well with cracked ice and
strain into 3 oz. cocktail glass.*

POKER COCKTAIL

1¼ oz. Sweet Vermouth
1¼ oz. Old Mr. Boston Imported
    Rum
*Stir well with cracked ice and strain
into 3 oz. cocktail glass.*

POLLYANNA COCKTAIL

*Muddle 3 slices of orange and
slices of pineapple*
2 oz. Old Mr. Boston Dry Gin
½ oz. Sweet Vermouth
½ Teaspoon Grenadine
*Shake well with cracked ice an
strain into 4 oz. cocktail glass.*

POLO COCKTAIL

½ oz. Lemon Juice
½ oz. Orange Juice
1 oz. Old Mr. Boston Dry Gin
*Shake well with cracked ice an
strain into 3 oz. cocktail glass.*

POLYNESIAN COCKTAIL

1½ oz. Old Mr. Boston Vodka
¾ oz. Old Mr. Boston Wild Cher.
    Flavored Brandy
Juice of 1 Lime
*Shake well with cracked ice an
strain into 4 oz. cocktail glass. Fr
rim by rubbing with lime and di*
ping in powdered sugar.

POOP DECK COCKTAIL

1¼ oz. Old Mr. Boston Blackber
    Flavored Brandy
½ oz. Port Wine
½ oz. Old Mr. Boston Five St
    Brandy
*Stir well with cracked ice and stra
into 3 oz. cocktail glass.*

POPPY COCKTAIL

¾ oz. Old Mr. Boston Creme
    Cacao
1½ oz. Old Mr. Boston Dry Gin
*Shake well with cracked ice a
strain into 3 oz. cocktail glass.*

Port and Starboard

½ oz. Grenadine
½ oz. Old Mr. Boston Creme de Menthe (green)
our carefully into Pousse Café lass, so that Menthe floats on Grendine.

Port Milk Punch

Teaspoon Powdered Sugar
oz. Port Wine
½ pt. Milk
hake well with cracked ice, strain nto 12 oz. Tom Collins glass and rate nutmeg on top.

Port Wine Cobbler

issolve 1 teaspoon powdered sugar n 2 oz. carbonated water; then fill 0 oz. goblet with shaved ice and add oz. Port Wine. *Stir well and decoate with fruits in season. Serve with traws.*

Port Wine Cocktail

¼ oz. Port Wine
Teaspoon Old Mr. Boston Five Star Brandy
tir slightly with cracked ice and rain into 3 oz. cocktail glass.

Port Wine Eggnog

Egg
Teaspoon Powdered Sugar
oz. Port Wine
ill glass with milk. Shake well with acked ice and strain into 12 oz. om Collins glass. Grate nutmeg on p.

Port Wine Flip

1 Egg
1 Teaspoon Powdered Sugar
1½ oz. Port Wine
2 Teaspoons Sweet Cream (if desired)
Shake well with cracked ice and strain into 5 oz. flip glass. Grate a little nutmeg on top.

Port Wine Negus

½ Lump Sugar
2 oz. Port Wine
Fill hot whiskey glass with hot water and stir. Grate nutmeg on top.

Port Wine Sangaree

Dissolve ½ teaspoon powdered sugar in 1 teaspoon of water.
2 oz. Port Wine
2 cubes of Ice
Serve in 8 oz. highball glass. Fill balance with soda water. Stir, leaving enough room on which to float a tablespoon of Brandy. Sprinkle lightly with nutmeg.

Pousse Café

⅙ Grenadine
⅙ Yellow Chartreuse
⅙ Creme de Yvette
⅙ Old Mr. Boston Creme de Menthe (white)
⅙ Green Chartreuse
⅙ Old Mr. Boston Five Star Brandy
Pour carefully, in order given, into Pousse Café glass so that each ingredient floats on preceding one.

See Index on page 145 for complete list of Pousse Café *recipes.*

Pousse L'Amour

⅓ oz. Maraschino
Yolk of 1 Egg
⅓ oz. Benedictine
⅓ oz. Old Mr. Boston Five Star Brandy
Pour carefully, in order given, into 2 oz. Sherry glass, so that each ingredient floats on preceding one.

Prairie Hen Cocktail

1 Whole Egg
1 Teaspoon Worcestershire Sauce
½ Teaspoon Vinegar
1 Drop Tabasco Sauce
Season with a little salt and pepper. Use 5 oz. Delmonico glass.

Prairie Oyster Cocktail

1 Whole Egg
1 Teaspoon Worcestershire Sauce
1 Teaspoon Tomato Catsup
½ Teaspoon Vinegar
Pinch of Pepper
1 Drop Tabasco Sauce
Use 5 oz. Delmonico glass.

Preakness Cocktail

¾ oz. Sweet Vermouth
1½ oz. Old Mr. Boston Whiskey*
1 Dash Bitters
½ Teaspoon Benedictine
Stir well with cracked ice and strain into 3 oz. cocktail glass. Add twist of lemon peel and drop in glass.

Presto Cocktail

½ oz. Orange Juice
½ oz. Sweet Vermouth
1¼ oz. Old Mr. Boston Five Star Brandy
¼ Teaspoon Absinthe Substitute
Shake well with cracked ice and strain into 3 oz. cocktail glass.

Prince's Smile Cocktail

½ oz. Old Mr. Boston Apricot Flavored Brandy
½ oz. Apple Brandy
1 oz. Old Mr. Boston Dry Gin
¼ Teaspoon Lemon Juice
Shake well with cracked ice and strain into 3 oz. cocktail glass.

Princess Pousse Cafe

¾ oz. Old Mr. Boston Apricot Flavored Brandy
¼ oz. Sweet Cream
Pour cream carefully on top, so that it does not mix. Use Pousse Cafe glass.

Princeton Cocktail

1 oz. Old Mr. Boston Dry Gin
1 oz. Dry Vermouth
Juice ½ Lime
Stir well with cracked ice and strain into 3 oz. cocktail glass.

Punches

See Index on page 145 for complete list of PUNCH recipes.

* Bourbon, Blended, Rye or Canadian

Quaker's Cocktail

¾ oz. Old Mr. Boston Imported Rum
¾ oz. Old Mr. Boston Five Star Brandy
Juice ¼ Lemon
2 Teaspoons Raspberry Syrup
Shake well with cracked ice and strain into 3 oz. cocktail glass.

Quarter Deck Cocktail

⅓ oz. Sherry Wine
1½ oz. Old Mr. Boston Imported Rum
Juice ½ Lime
Stir well with cracked ice and strain into 3 oz. cocktail glass.

Queen Charlotte

2 oz. Claret Wine
1 oz. Raspberry Syrup or Grenadine
Pour into 12 oz. Tom Collins glass. Add cub of ice; fill with lemon soda and stir.

Queen Elizabeth Cocktail

1½ oz. Old Mr. Boston Dry Gin
½ oz. Dry Vermouth
¼ oz. Benedictine
Stir well with cracked ice and strain into 3 oz. cocktail glass.

R

RACQUET CLUB COCKTAIL

1½ oz. Old Mr. Boston Dry Gin
¾ oz. Dry Vermouth
1 Dash Orange Bitters
Stir well with cracked ice and strain into 3 oz. cocktail glass.

RAMOS FIZZ

Juice ½ Lemon
White of 1 Egg
1 Teaspoon Powdered Sugar
2 oz. Old Mr. Boston Dry Gin
1 Tablespoon Sweet Cream
½ Teaspoon Orange Flower Water
Shake well with cracked ice and strain into 12 oz. Tom Collins glass. Fill with carbonated water and stir.

RATTLESNAKE COCKTAIL

1½ oz. Old Mr. Boston Whiskey*
White of 1 Egg
1 Teaspoon Lemon Juice
½ Teaspoon Powdered Sugar
¼ Teaspoon Absinthe Substitute
Shake well with cracked ice and strain into 4 oz. cocktail glass.

RED SWIZZLE

Make same as GIN SWIZZLE *(see pag 43), and add 1 tablespoon of grena dine. If desired, rum, brandy o whiskey may be substituted for the gin.*

REFORM COCKTAIL

¾ oz. Dry Vermouth
1½ oz. Sherry Wine
1 Dash Orange Bitters
Stir well with cracked ice and strain into 3 oz. cocktail glass. Serve with cherry.

REMSEN COOLER

Into 12 oz. Tom Collins glass, put:
½ Teaspoon Powdered Sugar
2 oz. Carbonated Water
Stir; fill glass with Cracked Ice an add:
2 oz. Old Mr. Boston Dry Gin
Fill with carbonated water or gi ger ale and stir again. Insert spira of orange or lemon peel (or both) an dangle end over rim of glass.

* Bourbon, Blended, Rye or Canadian

RESOLUTE COCKTAIL

Juice ¼ Lemon
½ oz. Old Mr. Boston Apricot Flavored Brandy
1 oz. Old Mr. Boston Dry Gin
Shake well with cracked ice and strain into 3 oz. cocktail glass.

RHINE WINE CUP

Use Large Glass Pitcher
4 Teaspoons Powdered Sugar
6 oz. Carbonated Water
½ oz. Triple Sec
½ oz. Curacao
2 oz. Old Mr. Boston Five Star Brandy
Fill pitcher with cubes of ice. Add 1 pint of Rhine wine. Stir well and decorate with as many fruits as available and also rind of cucumber inserted on each side of pitcher. Top with small bunch of mint sprigs. Serve in 5 oz. Claret glass.

RICKIES

See Index on page 145 for complete list of RICKEY recipes.

ROB ROY COCKTAIL

¾ oz. Sweet Vermouth
1½ oz. Old Mr. Boston Scotch Whisky
Dash Orange Bitters
Stir well with cracked ice and strain into 3 oz. cocktail glass.

ROBERT E. LEE COOLER

Into 12 oz. Tom Collins glass, put:
Juice ½ Lime
½ Teaspoon Powdered Sugar
2 oz. Carbonated Water, and stir
Fill glass with cracked ice and add:
¼ Teaspoon Absinthe Substitute
2 oz. Old Mr. Boston Dry Gin
Fill with ginger ale and stir again. Insert spiral of orange or lemon peel (or both) and dangle end over rim of glass.

ROBSON COCKTAIL

2 Teaspoons Lemon Juice
½ oz. Orange Juice
¼ oz. Grenadine
1 oz. Jamaica Rum
Shake well with cracked ice and strain into 3 oz. cocktail glass.

ROC-A-COE COCKTAIL

1¼ oz. Sherry Wine
1¼ oz. Old Mr. Boston Dry Gin
Stir well with cracked ice and strain into 3 oz. cocktail glass. Serve with a cherry.

ROLLS-ROYCE COCKTAIL

½ oz. Dry Vermouth
½ oz. Sweet Vermouth
1¼ oz. Old Mr. Boston Dry Gin
¼ Teaspoon Benedictine
Stir well with cracked ice and strain into 3 oz. cocktail glass.

ROMA COCKTAIL

1 oz. Old Mr. Boston Dry Gin
½ oz. Dry Vermouth
½ oz. Sweet Vermouth
Add 2 or 3 strawberries. Shake well with cracked ice and strain into 3 oz. cocktail glass.

Rory O'More

¾ oz. Sweet Vermouth
1½ oz. Irish Whiskey
1 Dash Orange Bitters
Stir well with cracked ice and strain into 3 oz. cocktail glass.

Rose Cocktail (English)

½ oz. Old Mr. Boston Apricot Flavored Brandy
½ oz. Dry Vermouth
1 oz. Old Mr. Boston Dry Gin
½ Teaspoon Lemon Juice
1 Teaspoon Grenadine
Shake well with cracked ice and strain into 3 oz. cocktail glass. Frost edge of glass by rubbing with lemon and dipping in powdered sugar.

Rose Cocktail (French)

½ oz. Old Mr. Boston Wild Cherry Flavored Brandy
½ oz. Dry Vermouth
1¼ oz. Old Mr. Boston Dry Gin
Stir well with cracked ice and strain into 3 oz. cocktail glass.

Roselyn Cocktail

¾ oz. Dry Vermouth
1½ oz. Old Mr. Boston Dry Gin
½ Teaspoon Grenadine
Stir well with cracked ice and strain into 3 oz. cocktail glass. Twist of lemon peel on top and drop in glass.

Royal Clover Club Cocktail

Juice 1 Lime
1 Tablespoon Grenadine
Yolk 1 Egg
1½ oz. Old Mr. Boston Dry Gin
Shake well with cracked ice and strain into 4 oz. cocktail glass.

Royal Cocktail

1 Whole Egg
Juice ½ Lemon
1 Teaspoon Powdered Sugar
1½ oz. Old Mr. Boston Dry Gin
Shake well with cracked ice an strain into 4 oz. cocktail glass.

Royal Fizz

Juice ½ Lemon
1 Teaspoon Powdered Sugar
2 oz. Old Mr. Boston Dry Gin
1 Whole Egg
Shake well with cracked ice an strain into 8 oz. highball glass. Fi with carbonated water and stir.

Royal Purple Punch

Pour 2 large bottles (⅘ quart size Claret Wine and 2 large bottles gin ger ale over ice cubes in punch bow. Stir well. Float thin slices of lemo studded with cloves on top. Serve i 4 oz. punch glasses.

Royal Smile Cocktail

Juice ¼ Lemon
1 Teaspoon Grenadine
½ oz. Old Mr. Boston Dry Gin
1 oz. Apple Brandy
Stir well with cracked ice and strai into 3 oz. cocktail glass.

Ruby Fizz

Juice ½ Lemon
1 Teaspoon Powdered Sugar
White of 1 Egg
1 Teaspoon Grenadine
2 oz. Old Mr. Boston Sloe Gin
Shake well with cracked ice an strain into 8 oz. highball glass. F with carbonated water and stir.

Rum Cobbler

Dissolve, in a 10 oz. goblet,
1 Teaspoon Powdered Sugar
2 oz. Carbonated Water
Fill goblet with shaved ice, and add:
2 oz. Old Mr. Boston Imported
 Rum
*Stir well and decorate with fruits in
season. Serve with straws.*

Rum Cola

See Cuba Libra *Page 29.*

Rum Collins

Juice 1 Lime
1 Teaspoon Powdered Sugar
2 oz. Old Mr. Boston Imported
 Rum
*Shake well with cracked ice and
strain into 12 oz. Tom Collins glass.
Add several cubes of ice, fill with carbonated water and stir. Decorate
with slice of lemon and a cherry and
drop lime in glass. Serve with
straws.*

Rum Cooler

Into 12 oz. Tom Collins glass, put:
½ Teaspoon Powdered Sugar
2 oz. Carbonated Water
*Stir; fill glass with cracked ice and
add:*
2 oz. Old Mr. Boston Imported
 Rum
*Fill with carbonated water or gin-
ger ale and stir again. Insert spiral
of orange or lemon peel (or both)
and dangle end over rim of glass.*

Rum Daisy

Juice of ½ Lemon
½ Teaspoon Powdered Sugar
1 Teaspoon Raspberry Syrup
 Grenadine
2 oz. Old Mr. Boston Imported
 Rum
*Shake well with cracked ice an
strain into Stein or 8 oz. metal cu
Add cube of ice and decorate wi
fruit.*

Rum Eggnog

1 Egg
1 Teaspoon Powdered Sugar
2 oz. Old Mr. Boston Imported
 Rum
*Fill glass with milk. Shake well wi
cracked ice and strain into 12 o
Tom Collins glass. Grate nutmeg o
top.*

Rum Fix

Juice ½ Lemon or 1 Lime
1 Teaspoon Powdered Sugar
1 Teaspoon Water and stir
Fill glass with Shaved Ice
2½ oz. Old Mr. Boston Import
 Rum
*Use 8 oz. highball glass. Stir we
Add slice of lemon. Serve wi
straws.*

Rum Highball

1 Cube of Ice
2 oz. Old Mr. Boston Importe
 Rum
*Fill 8 oz. highball glass with ging
ale or carbonated water. Add tw
of lemon peel, if desired, and stir.*

RUM MILK PUNCH

Teaspoon Powdered Sugar
oz. Old Mr. Boston Imported
Rum
2 pt. Milk
*Shake well with cracked ice, strain
into 12 oz. Tom Collins glass and
grate nutmeg on top.*

RUM RICKEY

Cube of Ice
Juice ½ Lime
1½ oz. Old Mr. Boston Imported
Rum
*Fill 8 oz. highball glass with carbon-
ated water and stir. Leave lime in
glass.*

RUM SOUR

Juice ½ Lemon
½ Teaspoon Powdered Sugar
2 oz. Old Mr. Boston Imported
Rum
*Shake well with cracked ice and
strain into 6 oz. sour glass. Fill with
carbonated water and stir. Decorate
with a half-slice of lemon and a
cherry.*

RUM SWIZZLE

*Made same as GIN SWIZZLE (see page
43), using 2 oz. Old Mr. Boston
Imported Rum.*

RUM TODDY

Use Old Fashioned cocktail glass.
½ Teaspoon Powdered Sugar
2 Teaspoons Water
Stir.
2 oz. Old Mr. Boston Imported
Rum
1 Lump of Ice
*Stir again and twist lemon peel on
top.*

RUM TODDY (Hot)

*Put lump of sugar into hot Whiskey
glass and fill two-thirds with boiling
water. Add 2 oz. Old Mr. Boston
Imported Rum. Stir and decorate
with slice of lemon. Grate nutmeg on
top.*

RUSSIAN BEAR COCKTAIL

1 oz. Old Mr. Boston Vodka
½ oz. Old Mr. Boston Creme de
Cacao
½ oz. Sweet Cream
*Stir well with cracked ice and strain
into 3 oz. cocktail glass.*

RUSSIAN COCKTAIL

¾ oz. Old Mr. Boston Creme de
Cacao
¾ oz. Old Mr. Boston Dry Gin
¾ oz. Old Mr. Boston Vodka
*Shake well with cracked ice and
strain into 3 oz. cocktail glass.*

RYE HIGHBALL

1 Cube of Ice
2 oz. Old Mr. Boston Rye Whiskey
*Fill 8 oz. highball glass with ginger
ale or carbonated water. Add twist
of lemon peel, if desired, and stir.*

RYE WHISKEY COCKTAIL

1 Dash Bitters
1 Teaspoon Simple Syrup
2 oz. Old Mr. Boston Rye Whiskey
*Stir well with cracked ice and strain
into 3 oz. cocktail glass. Serve with a
cherry.*

St. Patrick's Day Cocktail

¾ oz. Old Mr. Boston Creme de Menthe (green)
¾ oz. Green Chartreuse
¾ oz. Irish Whiskey
1 Dash Bitters
Stir well with cracked ice and strain into 3 oz. cocktail glass.

Salty Dog

Fill 12 oz. Tom Collins glass almost full with shaved ice or ice cubes and add:
2 oz. Old Mr. Boston Dry Gin
4 oz. Grapefruit Juice
Add pinch of salt and stir well.

San Francisco Cocktail

¾ oz. Old Mr. Boston Sloe Gin
¾ oz. Sweet Vermouth
¾ oz. Dry Vermouth
1 Dash Bitters
1 Dash Orange Bitters
Shake well with cracked ice and strain into 3 oz. cocktail glass. Serve with a cherry.

Sand-Martin Cocktail

1 Teaspoon Green Chartreuse
1¼ oz. Sweet Vermouth
1¼ oz. Old Mr. Boston Dry Gin
Stir well with cracked ice and strain into 3 oz. cocktail glass.

Sangarees

See Index on page 146 for complete list of SANGAREE recipes.

Santiago Cocktail

½ Teaspoon Powdered Sugar
¼ Teaspoon Grenadine
Juice 1 Lime
1½ oz. Old Mr. Boston Imported Rum
Shake well with cracked ice and strain into 3 oz. cocktail glass.

Saratoga Cocktail

2 oz. Old Mr. Boston Five Star Brandy
2 Dashes Bitters
½ Teaspoon Pineapple Syrup
½ Teaspoon Maraschino
Stir well with cracked ice and strain into 3 oz. cocktail glass.

Saratoga Cooler

Fill 12 oz. Tom Collins glass with cracked ice. Fill with sarsaparilla. Insert spiral of lemon and dangle end over rim of glass.

SAUCY SUE COCKTAIL

2 Teaspoon Old Mr. Boston
    Apricot Flavored Brandy
2 Teaspoon Absinthe Substitute
 oz. Apple Brandy
*Stir well with cracked ice and strain
into 3 oz. cocktail glass.*

SAUTERNE CUP

Use large glass pitcher.
Teaspoons Powdered Sugar
 oz. Carbonated Water
 oz. Triple Sec
 oz. Curacao
 oz. Old Mr. Boston Five Star
    Brandy
*Fill pitcher with cubes of ice. Add 1
pint of Sauterne. Stir well and decorate with as many fruits as available
and also rind of cucumber inserted
in each side of pitcher. Top with
small bunch of mint sprigs. Serve in
4 oz. Claret glass.*

SAXON COCKTAIL

Juice ½ Lime
 Teaspoon Grenadine
¾ oz. Old Mr. Boston Imported
    Rum
Twist Orange Peel
*Shake well with cracked ice and
strain into 3 oz. cocktail glass.*

SAZERAC COCKTAIL

*Put ¼ Teaspoon Absinthe Substitute
into an Old Fashioned cocktail glass
and revolve glass until it is entirely
coated with the Absinthe Substitute.
Then add:*
½ Lump of Sugar
2 Dashes Bitters
*Sufficient water to cover sugar, and
muddle well.*
2 Cubes of Ice
2 oz. Old Mr. Boston Whiskey*
*Stir very well. Add twist of lemon
peel. (For best results, put glass on
ice for a few minutes before using.)*

SCOTCH BISHOP COCKTAIL

1 oz. Old Mr. Boston Scotch
    Whisky
½ oz. Orange Juice
½ oz. Dry Vermouth
½ Teaspoon Triple Sec
¼ Teaspoon Powdered Sugar
Twist of Lemon Peel
*Shake well with cracked ice and
strain into 3 oz. cocktail glass.*

SCOTCH COOLER

2 oz. Old Mr. Boston Scotch
    Whisky
3 Dashes Old Mr. Boston Creme de
    Menthe (white)
*Stir into 8 oz. highball glass with ice
cubes. Fill with chilled carbonated
water and stir.*

SCOTCH MILK PUNCH

2 oz. Old Mr. Boston Scotch
    Whisky
6 oz. Milk
Teaspoon powdered sugar
*Shake thoroughly with cracked ice.
Pour into 12 oz. Tom Collins glass.
Sprinkle with nutmeg.*

*Bourbon, Blended, Rye or Canadian.

Scotch Mist

*Fill Old Fashioned cocktail glass
with shaved ice. Pour in* Old Mr.
Boston Scotch Whisky. *Add twist
of lemon peel. Serve with short
straws.*

Scotch Old Fashioned

Make same as Old Fashioned
Cocktail *(See page 68), except sub-
stitute* Old Mr. Boston Scotch
Whisky.

Scotch Rickey

1 Cube of Ice
Juice ½ Lime
1½ oz. Old Mr. Boston Scotch
Whisky
*Fill 8 oz. highball glass with carbon-
ated water and stir. Leave lime in
glass.*

Scotch Sour

1½ oz. Old Mr. Boston Scotch
Whisky
Juice of ½ Lime
½ Teaspoon Powdered Sugar
*Shake well with cracked ice; strain
into 6 oz. sour glass. Fill with carbonated water and stir. Decorate
with orange slices and cherry.*

Scotch Whisky Highball

1 Cube of Ice
2 oz. Old Mr. Boston Scotch
Whisky
*Fill 8 oz. highball glass with ginger
ale or carbonated water. Add twist
of lemon peel, if desired, and stir.*

Screwdriver

*Put 2 or 3 cubes of ice into 6 oz. glass.
Add 2 oz.* Old Mr. Boston Vodka.
*Fill balance of glass with orange
juice and stir.*

Sensation Cocktail

Juice of ¼ Lemon
1½ oz. Old Mr. Boston Dry Gin
1 Teaspoon Maraschino
3 Sprigs Fresh Mint
*Shake well with cracked ice and
strain into 3 oz. cocktail glass.*

September Morn Cocktail

White of 1 Egg
1½ oz. Old Mr. Boston Imported
Rum
Juice of ½ Lime
1 Teaspoon Grenadine
*Shake well with cracked ice and
strain into 4 oz. cocktail glass.*

Seventh Heaven Cocktail

2 Teaspoons Grapefruit Juice
½ oz. Maraschino
1¼ oz. Old Mr. Boston Dry Gin
*Shake well with cracked ice and
strain into 3 oz. cocktail glass. Decorate with sprig of fresh mint.*

Sevilla Cocktail

½ Teaspoon Powdered Sugar
1 Egg
1 oz. Port Wine
1 oz. Old Mr. Boston Imported
Rum
*Shake well with cracked ice and
strain into 4 oz. cocktail glass.*

SHAMROCK COCKTAIL

½ oz. Irish Whiskey
½ oz. Dry Vermouth
1 Teaspoon Old Mr. Boston
  Creme de Menthe (green)
*Stir well with cracked ice and strain
into 3 oz. cocktail glass. Serve with
an olive.*

SHANDY GAFF

6 oz. Beer
6 oz. Ginger Ale
*Use 12 oz. Tom Collins glass and
stir very gently.*

SHANGHAI COCKTAIL

Juice ¼ Lemon
1 Teaspoon Old Mr. Boston
  Anisette
1 oz. Jamaica Rum
½ Teaspoon Grenadine
*Shake well with cracked ice and
strain into 3 oz. cocktail glass.*

SHERRY AND EGG COCKTAIL

*Place an egg in a glass, being care-
ful not to break the yolk. Fill glass
with Sherry. Use 4 oz. cocktail glass.*

SHERRY COBBLER

Dissolve:
1 Teaspoon Powdered Sugar
2 oz. Carbonated Water
Fill goblet with shaved ice; add:
4 oz. Sherry Wine
*Stir well and decorate with fruits in
season. Serve with straws.*

SHERRY COCKTAIL

2½ oz. Sherry Wine
1 Dash Bitters
*Stir well with cracked ice and strain
into 3 oz. cocktail glass. Twist of
orange peel and drop in glass.*

SHERRY EGGNOG

1 Egg
1 Teaspoon Powdered Sugar
3 oz. Sherry Wine
*Fill glass with milk. Shake well with
cracked ice and strain into 12 oz.
Tom Collins glass. Grate nutmeg on
top.*

SHERRY FLIP

1 Egg
1 Teaspoon Powdered Sugar
1½ oz. Sherry Wine
2 Teaspoons Sweet Cream
  (if desired)
*Shake well with cracked ice and
strain into 5 oz. flip glass. Grate a
little nutmeg on top.*

SHERRY MILK PUNCH

1 Teaspoon Powdered Sugar
3 oz. Sherry Wine
½ pt. Milk
*Shake well with cracked ice, strain
into 12 oz. Tom Collins glass and
grate nutmeg on top.*

SHERRY SANGAREE

Dissolve ½ teaspoon powdered sugar in 1 teaspoon of water. Add:
2 oz. Sherry Wine
2 cubes of Ice
Serve in 8 oz. highball glass. Fill balance with soda water. Stir, leaving enough room on which to float a tablespoon of Port Wine. *Sprinkle lightly with nutmeg.*

SHERRY TWIST COCKTAIL

1 oz. Sherry Wine
⅓ oz. Old Mr. Boston Five Star Brandy
⅓ oz. Dry Vermouth
⅓ oz. Triple Sec
½ Teaspoon Lemon Juice
Shake well with cracked ice and strain into 3 oz. cocktail glass. Top with pinch of cinnamon and twist of orange peel dropped in glass.

SHRINER COCKTAIL

1¼ oz. Old Mr. Boston Five Star Brandy
1¼ oz. Old Mr. Boston Sloe Gin
2 Dashes Bitters
½ Teaspoon Simple Syrup
Stir well with cracked ice and strain into 3 oz. cocktail glass. Twist of lemon peel and drop into glass.

SIDECAR COCKTAIL

Juice ¼ Lemon
½ oz. Triple Sec
1 oz. Old Mr. Boston Five Star Brandy
Shake well with cracked ice and strain into 3 oz. cocktail glass.

SILVER COCKTAIL

1 oz. Dry Vermouth
1 oz. Old Mr. Boston Dry Gin
2 Dashes Orange Bitters
¼ Teaspoon Simple Syrup
½ Teaspoon Maraschino
Stir well with cracked ice and strain into 3 oz. cocktail glass. Twist of lemon peel and drop into glass.

SILVER FIZZ

Juice ½ Lemon
1 Teaspoon Powdered Sugar
2 oz. Old Mr. Boston Dry Gin
White of 1 Egg
Shake well with cracked ice and strain into 8 oz. highball glass. Fill with carbonated water and stir.

SILVER KING COCKTAIL

White of 1 Egg
Juice ¼ Lemon
1½ oz. Old Mr. Boston Dry Gin
½ Teaspoon Powdered Sugar
2 Dashes Orange Bitters
Shake well with cracked ice and strain into 4 oz. cocktail glass.

SILVER STALLION FIZZ

1 Scoop Vanilla Ice Cream
2 oz. Old Mr. Boston Dry Gin
Use 8 oz. highball glass; fill with carbonated water and stir.

S

SINGAPORE SLING

Juice ½ Lemon
Teaspoon Powdered Sugar
oz. Old Mr. Boston Dry Gin
oz. Old Mr. Boston Wild Cherry
Flavored Brandy
*Shake well with cracked ice and
strain into 12 oz. Tom Collins glass.
Add ice cubes and fill with carbonated water; stir. Decorate with fruits
in season and serve with straws.*

SIR WALTER COCKTAIL

oz. Old Mr. Boston Imported
Rum
oz. Old Mr. Boston Five Star
Brandy
Teaspoon Grenadine
Teaspoon Curacao
Teaspoon Lemon Juice
*Shake well with cracked ice and
strain into 3 oz. cocktail glass.*

SKYROCKET COCKTAIL

oz. Old Mr. Boston Whiskey*
oz. Dry Vermouth
oz. Swedish Punch
Dash Bitters
Teaspoon Lemon Juice
*Shake well with cracked ice and
strain into 3 oz. cocktail glass.*

SLINGS

*See Index on page 146 for complete
list of SLING recipes.*

SLOE GIN COCKTAIL

oz. Old Mr. Boston Sloe Gin
Dash Orange Bitters
Teaspoon Dry Vermouth
*Stir well with cracked ice and strain
into 3 oz. cocktail glass.*

SLOE GIN COLLINS

Juice ½ Lemon
2 oz. Old Mr. Boston Sloe Gin
*Shake well with cracked ice and
strain into 12 oz. Tom Collins glass.
Add several cubes of ice, fill with carbonated water and stir. Decorate
with slice of lemon, orange and a
cherry. Serve with straws.*

SLOE GIN FIZZ

Juice of ½ Lemon
1 Teaspoon Powdered Sugar
2 oz. Old Mr. Boston Sloe Gin
*Shake well with cracked ice and
strain into 8 oz. highball glass. Fill
with carbonated water and stir. Decorate with slice of lemon.*

SLOE GIN FLIP

1 Egg
1 Teaspoon Powdered Sugar
½ oz. Old Mr. Boston Sloe Gin
2 Teaspoons Sweet Cream
(if desired)
*Shake well with cracked ice and
strain into 5 oz. flip glass. Grate a
little nutmeg on top.*

SLOE GIN RICKEY

1 Cube of Ice
Juice of ½ Lime
2 oz. Old Mr. Boston Sloe Gin
*Fill 8 oz. highball glass with carbon-
ated water and stir. Leave Lime in
glass.*

SLOEBERRY COCKTAIL

1 Dash Bitters
2 oz. Old Mr. Boston Sloe Gin
*Stir well with cracked ice and strain
into 3 oz. cocktail glass.*

Bourbon, Blended, Rye or Canadian.

Sloppy Joe's Cocktail No. 1

Juice 1 Lime
¼ Teaspoon Curacao
¼ Teaspoon Grenadine
¾ oz. Old Mr. Boston Imported Rum
¾ oz. Dry Vermouth
Shake well with cracked ice and strain into 3 oz. cocktail glass.

Sloppy Joe's Cocktail No. 2

¾ oz. Pineapple Juice
¾ oz. Old Mr. Boston Five Star Brandy
¾ oz. Port Wine
¼ Teaspoon Curacao
¼ Teaspoon Grenadine
Shake well with cracked ice and strain into 3 oz. cocktail glass.

Smashes

See Index on page 146 for complete list of SMASH recipes.

Smile Cocktail

1 oz. Grenadine
1 oz. Old Mr. Boston Dry Gin
½ Teaspoon Lemon Juice
Shake well with cracked ice and strain into 3 oz. cocktail glass.

Smiler Cocktail

½ oz. Sweet Vermouth
½ oz. Dry Vermouth
1 oz. Old Mr. Boston Dry Gin
1 Dash Bitters
¼ Teaspoon Orange Juice
Shake well with cracked ice and strain into 3 oz. cocktail glass.

Snowball Cocktail

1½ oz. Old Mr. Boston Dry Gin
½ oz. Old Mr. Boston Anisette
½ oz. Sweet Cream
Shake well with cracked ice and strain into 4 oz. cocktail glass.

Society Cocktail

1½ oz. Old Mr. Boston Dry Gin
¾ oz. Dry Vermouth
¼ Teaspoon Grenadine
Stir well with cracked ice and strain into 3 oz. cocktail glass.

Soother Cocktail

½ oz. Old Mr. Boston Five Star Brandy
½ oz. Apple Brandy
½ oz. Curacao
Juice ½ Lemon
1 Teaspoon Powdered Sugar
Shake well with cracked ice and strain into 3 oz. cocktail glass.

Soul Kiss Cocktail

¼ oz. Orange Juice
¼ oz. Dubonnet
¾ oz. Dry Vermouth
¾ oz. Old Mr. Boston Whiskey*
Shake well with cracked ice and strain into 3 oz. cocktail glass.

Sours

See Index on page 146 for complete list of SOUR recipes.

Sourteq

See TEQUILA SOUR on page 97.

* *Bourbon, Blended, Rye or Canadian*

South Side Cocktail

Juice ½ Lemon
1 Teaspoon Powdered Sugar
2 Sprigs Fresh Mint
1½ oz. Old Mr. Boston Dry Gin
Shake well with cracked ice and strain into 3 oz. cocktail glass.

South Side Fizz

Juice ½ Lemon
1 Teaspoon Powdered Sugar
2 oz. Old Mr. Boston Dry Gin
Shake well with cracked ice and strain into 7 oz. highball glass. Fill with carbonated water and stir. Add fresh mint leaves.

Southern Gin Cocktail

2 oz. Old Mr. Boston Dry Gin
2 Dashes Orange Bitters
½ Teaspoon Curacao
Stir well with cracked ice and strain into 3 oz. cocktail glass. Twist of lemon peel and drop into glass.

Spanish Town Cocktail

2 oz. Old Mr. Boston Imported Rum
1 Teaspoon Curacao
Stir well with cracked ice and strain into 3 oz. cocktail glass.

Special Rough Cocktail

¾ oz. Apple Brandy
¾ oz. Old Mr. Boston Five Star Brandy
¼ Teaspoon Absinthe Substitute
Stir well with cracked ice and strain into 3 oz. cocktail glass.

Spencer Cocktail

¾ oz. Old Mr. Boston Apricot Flavored Brandy
1½ oz. Old Mr. Boston Dry Gin
1 Dash Bitters
¼ Teaspoon Orange Juice
Shake well with cracked ice and strain into 3 oz. cocktail glass. Add a cherry and twist of orange peel.

Sphinx Cocktail

1½ oz. Old Mr. Boston Dry Gin
¼ oz. Sweet Vermouth
¼ oz. Dry Vermouth
Stir well with cracked ice and strain into 3 oz. cocktail glass. Serve with slice of lemon on top.

Spring Feeling Cocktail

½ oz. Lemon Juice
½ oz. Green Chartreuse
1 oz. Old Mr. Boston Dry Gin
Shake well with cracked ice and strain into 3 oz. cocktail glass.

Spritzer Highball

Pour 3 oz. chilled Rhine Wine or Sauterne into 8 oz. highball glass with ice cubes. Fill balance with carbonated water and stir gently.

Stanley Cocktail

Juice ¼ Lemon
1 Teaspoon Grenadine
¾ oz. Old Mr. Boston Dry Gin
¾ oz. Old Mr. Boston Imported Rum
Shake well with cracked ice and strain into 3 oz. cocktail glass.

Star Cocktail

1 oz. Apple Brandy
1 oz. Sweet Vermouth
1 Dash Bitters
Stir well with cracked ice and strain into 3 oz. cocktail glass. Twist of lemon peel and drop into glass.

Star Daisy

Juice ½ Lemon
½ Teaspoon Powdered Sugar
1 Teaspoon Raspberry Syrup or Grenadine
1 oz. Old Mr. Boston Dry Gin
1 oz. Apple Brandy
Shake well with cracked ice and strain into stein or 8 oz. metal cup. Add cube of ice and decorate with fruit.

Stars and Stripes

⅓ Grenadine
⅓ Heavy Sweet Cream
⅓ Creme de Yvette
Pour carefully, in order given, into Pousse Café glass, so that each ingredient floats on preceding one.

Stinger Cocktail

1 oz. Old Mr. Boston Creme de Menthe (white)
1 oz. Old Mr. Boston Five Star Brandy
Shake well with cracked ice and strain into 3 oz. cocktail glass.

Stone Cocktail

½ oz. Old Mr. Boston Imported Rum
½ oz. Sweet Vermouth
1 oz. Sherry Wine
Stir well with cracked ice and strain into 3 oz. cocktail glass.

Stone Fence

1 Cube of Ice
2 Dashes Bitters
2 oz. Old Mr. Boston Scotch Whisky
Use 8 oz. highball glass and fill with carbonated water or cider and stir.

Straight Law Cocktail

¾ oz. Old Mr. Boston Dry Gin
1½ oz. Sherry Wine
Stir well with cracked ice and strain into 3 oz. cocktail glass.

Suissesse Cocktail

1½ oz. Absinthe Substitute
½ oz. Old Mr. Boston Anisette
White of 1 Egg
Shake well with cracked ice and strain into 4 oz. cocktail glass.

Sunshine Cocktail

¾ oz. Sweet Vermouth
1½ oz. Old Mr. Boston Dry Gin
1 Dash Bitters
Stir well with cracked ice and strain into 3 oz. cocktail glass. Twist of orange peel and drop into glass.

Susie Taylor

Juice ½ Lime
2 Cubes of Ice
2 oz. Old Mr. Boston Imported Rum
Fill 12 oz. Tom Collins glass with ginger ale and stir gently.

SWEET PATOOTIE COCKTAIL

1 oz. Old Mr. Boston Dry Gin
½ oz. Cointreau
½ oz. Orange Juice
Shake well with cracked ice and strain into 3 oz. cocktail glass.

SWISS FAMILY COCKTAIL

½ Teaspoon Absinthe Substitute
2 Dashes Bitters
¾ oz. Dry Vermouth
1½ oz. Old Mr. Boston Whiskey*
Stir well with cracked ice and strain into 3 oz. cocktail glass.

SWIZZLES

See Index on page 147 for complete list of SWIZZLE *recipes.*

TAILSPIN COCKTAIL

¾ oz. Old Mr. Boston Dry Gin
¾ oz. Sweet Vermouth
¾ oz. Green Chartreuse
1 Dash Orange Bitters
Stir well with cracked ice and strain into 3 oz. cocktail glass. Twist of lemon peel and serve with cherry or olive.

TANGO COCKTAIL

½ oz. Orange Juice
½ oz. Dry Vermouth
½ oz. Sweet Vermouth
1 oz. Old Mr. Boston Dry Gin
½ Teaspoon Curacao
Shake well with cracked ice and strain into 4 oz. cocktail glass.

TEMPTATION COCKTAIL

1½ oz. Old Mr. Boston Whiskey*
½ Teaspoon Curacao
½ Teaspoon Absinthe Substitute
½ Teaspoon Dubonnet
1 Twist Orange Peel
1 Twist Lemon Peel
Shake well with cracked ice and strain into 3 oz. cocktail glass.

TEMPTER COCKTAIL

1 oz. Port Wine
1 oz. Old Mr. Boston Apricot Flavored Brandy
Stir well with cracked ice and strain into 3 oz. cocktail glass.

* *Bourbon, Blended, Rye or Canadian*

TEQUILA COLLINS

Same as TOM COLLINS *(see page 100) except use Tequila instead of Dry Gin.*

TEQUILA SOUR

Juice ½ Lemon
1 Teaspoon Powdered Sugar
2 oz. Tequila
Shake well with cracked ice and strain into 6 oz. Sour glass. Fill with carbonated water. Decorate with half slice of lemon and a cherry.

TEQUILA STRAIGHT

½ Lemon
Pinch of Salt
Jigger Tequila
First suck lemon, place salt on tongue, then swallow Tequila.

TEQUINI COCKTAIL

1½ oz. Tequila
½ oz. Dry Vermouth
Dash Bitters may be added
Stir well with cracked ice and strain into 3 oz. cocktail glass. Serve with twist of lemon peel and an olive.

TEQUONIC

2 oz. Tequila
Juice of ½ Lemon or Lime
Pour Tequila over ice cubes in Old Fashioned cocktail glass. Add fruit juice; fill with tonic water and stir.

THANKSGIVING SPECIAL COCKTAIL

¾ oz. Old Mr. Boston Apricot
   Flavored Brandy
¾ oz. Old Mr. Boston Dry Gin
¾ oz. Dry Vermouth
¼ Teaspoon Lemon Juice
Shake well with cracked ice and strain into 3 oz. cocktail glass. Serve with a cherry.

THIRD DEGREE COCKTAIL

1½ oz. Old Mr. Boston Dry Gin
¾ oz. Dry Vermouth
1 Teaspoon Absinthe Substitute
Stir well with cracked ice and strain into 3 oz. cocktail glass.

THIRD RAIL COCKTAIL

¾ oz. Old Mr. Boston Imported
   Rum
¾ oz. Apple Brandy
¾ oz. Old Mr. Boston Five Star
   Brandy
¼ Teaspoon Absinthe Substitute
Stir well with cracked ice and strain into 3 oz. cocktail glass.

THISTLE COCKTAIL

1¼ oz. Sweet Vermouth
1¼ oz. Old Mr. Boston Scotch
   Whisky
2 Dashes Bitters
Stir well with cracked ice and strain into 3 oz. cocktail glass.

THREE MILLER COCKTAIL

¼ oz. Old Mr. Boston Imported
   Rum
¾ oz. Old Mr. Boston Five Star
   Brandy
1 Teaspoon Grenadine
¼ Teaspoon Lemon Juice
Shake well with cracked ice and
strain into 3 oz. cocktail glass.

THREE STRIPES COCKTAIL

1 oz. Old Mr. Boston Dry Gin
½ oz. Dry Vermouth
½ oz. Orange Juice
Shake well with cracked ice and
strain into 3 oz. cocktail glass.

THUNDER COCKTAIL

1 Teaspoon Powdered Sugar
Yolk of 1 Egg
1½ oz. Old Mr. Boston Five Star
   Brandy
1 Pinch of Cayenne Pepper
Shake well with cracked ice and
strain into 4 oz. cocktail glass.

THUNDER AND LIGHTNING
COCKTAIL

Yolk of 1 Egg
1 Teaspoon Powdered Sugar
1½ oz. Old Mr. Boston Five Star
   Brandy
Shake well with cracked ice and
strain into 4 oz. cocktail glass.

THUNDERCLAP COCKTAIL

1 oz. Old Mr. Boston Dry Gin
1 oz. Old Mr. Boston Whiskey*
1 oz. Old Mr. Boston Five Star
   Brandy
Stir well with cracked ice and strain
into 3 oz. cocktail glass.

*Bourbon, Blended, Rye or Canadian.

Ginger Flavored Brandy 70 Proof ▶
Flavored Brandy (Blackberry, Peach,
Apricot and Cherry) 70 Proof

TIPPERARY COCKTAIL

¾ oz. Irish Whiskey
¾ oz. Green Chartreuse
¾ oz. Sweet Vermouth
*Stir well with cracked ice and strain
into 3 oz. cocktail glass.*

T. N. T. COCKTAIL

1¼ oz. Old Mr. Boston Whiskey*
1¼ oz. Absinthe Substitute
*Stir well with cracked ice and strain
into 3 oz. cocktail glass.*

TODDIES

*See Index on page 147 for complete
list of* TODDY *recipes.*

TOM AND JERRY

*First prepare batter, using mixing
bowl. Separate the yolk and white of
1 egg, beating each separately and
thoroughly. Then combine both, adding enough superfine powdered sugar
to stiffen.* Add to this 1 pinch of baking soda and ¼ oz. Old Mr. Boston
Imported Rum *to preserve the batter.
Then add a little more sugar to
stiffen. To serve, use hot Tom and
Jerry mug, using 1 tablespoon of
above batter, dissolved in 3 table-
spoons hot milk. Add* 1½ oz. Old
Mr. Boston Imported Rum. *Then
fill mug with hot milk within ¼ inch
of top of mug and stir gently. Then
top with* ½ oz. Old Mr. Boston Five
Star Brandy *and grate a little nutmeg on top.*

*The secret of a Tom and Jerry is to
have a stiff batter and a warm mug.*

TOM COLLINS

Juice of ½ Lemon
1 Teaspoon Powdered Sugar
2 oz. Old Mr. Boston Dry Gin
*Shake well with cracked ice an
strain into 12 oz. Tom Collins glass
Add several cubes of ice, fill wit
carbonated water and stir. Decorat
with slice of lemon, orange and
cherry. Serve with straws.*

TOVARICH COCKTAIL

1½ oz. Old Mr. Boston Vodka
¾ oz. Old Mr. Boston Kummel
Juice of ½ Lime
*Shake well with cracked ice an
strain into 3 oz. cocktail glass.*

TRILBY COCKTAIL

1½ oz. Old Mr. Boston Whiskey*
¾ oz. Sweet Vermouth
2 Dashes Orange Bitters
*Stir well with cracked ice and strai
into 3 oz. cocktail glass.*

TRINITY COCKTAIL

¾ oz. Sweet Vermouth
¾ oz. Dry Vermouth
¾ oz. Old Mr. Boston Dry Gin
*Stir well with cracked ice and strai
into 3 oz. cocktail glass.*

TROPICAL COCKTAIL

¾ oz. Old Mr. Boston Creme de
Cacao
¾ oz. Maraschino
¾ oz. Dry Vermouth
1 Dash Bitters
*Stir well with cracked ice and strai
into 3 oz. cocktail glass.*

* *Bourbon, Blended, Rye or Canadia*

TULIP COCKTAIL

¼ oz. Lemon Juice
¼ oz. Old Mr. Boston Apricot
Flavored Brandy
¾ oz. Sweet Vermouth
¾ oz. Apple Brandy
Shake well with cracked ice and strain into 3 oz. cocktail glass.

TURF COCKTAIL

¼ Teaspoon Absinthe Substitute
2 Dashes Bitters
1 oz. Dry Vermouth
1 oz. Old Mr. Boston Dry Gin
Stir well with cracked ice and strain into 3 oz. cocktail glass. Twist of orange peel and drop in glass.

TUXEDO COCKTAIL

1¼ oz. Old Mr. Boston Dry Gin
1¼ oz. Dry Vermouth
¼ Teaspoon Maraschino
¼ Teaspoon Absinthe Substitute
2 Dashes Orange Bitters
Stir well with cracked ice and strain into 3 oz. cocktail glass. Serve with a cherry.

TWIN SIX COCKTAIL

1 oz. Old Mr. Boston Dry Gin
½ oz. Sweet Vermouth
¼ Teaspoon Grenadine
½ oz. Orange Juice
White of 1 Egg
Shake well with cracked ice and strain into 4 oz. cocktail glass.

TWISTER

2 oz. Old Mr. Boston Vodka
Juice of ⅓ Lime
Pour into 12 oz. Tom Collins glass. Add several cubes of ice, drop rind into glass. Fill with Seven-Up and stir well.

ULANDA COCKTAIL

1½ oz. Old Mr. Boston Dry Gin
¾ oz. Triple Sec
¼ Teaspoon Absinthe Substitute
Stir well with cracked ice and strain into 3 oz. cocktail glass.

UNION JACK COCKTAIL

¾ oz. Creme de Yvette
1½ oz. Old Mr. Boston Dry Gin
½ Teaspoon Grenadine
Shake well with cracked ice and strain into 3 oz. cocktail glass.

V

VALENCIA COCKTAIL

2 oz. Orange Juice
½ oz. Old Mr. Boston Apricot
   Flavored Brandy
Dashes Orange Bitters
*Shake well with cracked ice and
strain into 3 oz. cocktail glass.*

VANDERBILT COCKTAIL

1 oz. Old Mr. Boston Wild Cherry
   Flavored Brandy
½ oz. Old Mr. Boston Five Star
   Brandy
Teaspoon Simple Syrup
Dashes Bitters
*Stir well with cracked ice and strain
into 3 oz. cocktail glass.*

VERMOUTH CASSIS

1 oz. Creme de Cassis
2 oz. Dry Vermouth
Cube of Ice
*Fill 8 oz. highball glass with carbon-
ated water and stir.*

VERMOUTH COCKTAIL

1 oz. Dry Vermouth
1 oz. Sweet Vermouth
Dash Orange Bitters
*Stir well with cracked ice and strain
into 3 oz. cocktail glass. Serve with a
cherry.*

VIOLET FIZZ

Juice ½ Lemon
½ Teaspoon Powdered Sugar
1½ oz. Old Mr. Boston Dry Gin
½ oz. Creme de Yvette
*Shake well with cracked ice and
strain into 7 oz. highball glass. Fill
with carbonated water and stir.*

VODKA AND APPLE JUICE

*Put 2 or 3 cubes of ice into 6 oz. glass.
Add 2 oz. Old Mr. Boston Vodka.
Fill balance of glass with apple juice
and stir.*

VODKA AND TONIC

2 oz. Old Mr. Boston Vodka
Cube of Ice
*Use 12 oz. Tom Collins glass and
fill balance with quinine tonic and
stir.*

VODKA BLOODY MARY COCKTAIL

See BLOODY MARY COCKTAIL *on
page 10.*

VODKA COLLINS

Same as TOM COLLINS *(see page
100) except use* Old Mr. Boston
Vodka *instead of dry gin.*

(Cordials) Creme de Cacao 54 Proof White and Brown
         Creme de Menthe 60 Proof White and Green
         Kummel 70 Proof
         Anisette 60 Proof

VODKA COOLER

Same as GIN COOLER *(see page 40), except use* Old Mr. Boston Vodka *instead of gin.*

VODKA DAISY

Juice ½ Lemon
½ Teaspoon Powdered Sugar
1 Teaspoon Grenadine
2 oz. Old Mr. Boston Vodka
Shake well with cracked ice and strain into stein or 8 oz. metal cup. Add cube of ice and decorate with fruit.

VODKA GIBSON COCKTAIL

See GIBSON COCKTAIL *on page 117.*

VODKA GIMLET COCKTAIL

1½ oz. Old Mr. Boston Vodka
Juice ½ Lime
Stir well with cracked ice and strain into 3 oz. cocktail glass.

VODKA GRASSHOPPER COCKTAIL

¾ oz. Old Mr. Boston Vodka
¾ oz. Old Mr. Boston Creme de Menthe (green)
¾ oz. Old Mr. Boston Creme de Cacao (white)
Shake well with cracked ice, strain into 3 oz. cocktail glass.

VODKA GYPSY COCKTAIL

1½ oz. Old Mr. Boston Vodka
¾ oz. Benedictine
1 Dash Bitters
Stir well with cracked ice and strain into 3 oz. cocktail glass.

VODKA MARTINI COCKTAIL

See *Special Martini Section* on pages 116 and 117.

VODKA ON THE ROCKS

Put 2 or 3 ice cubes in Old Fashioned glass and add 2 oz. Old Mr. Boston Vodka. Serve with a twist of lemon peel.

VODKA "7"

2 oz. Old Mr. Boston Vodka
Juice ½ Lime
Use 12 oz. Tom Collins glass with cubes of ice. Drop lime in glass, fill balance with 7-Up and stir.

VODKA SLING

Same as GIN SLING *(See page 42) except use* Old Mr. Boston Vodka *instead of gin.*

VODKA SOUR

Juice ½ Lemon
½ Teaspoon Powdered Sugar
2 oz. Old Mr. Boston Vodka
Shake well with cracked ice and strain into 6 oz. sour glass. Fill with carbonated water and stir. Decorate with half-slice of lemon and a cherry.

VODKA STINGER

1 oz. Old Mr. Boston Vodka
1 oz. Old Mr. Boston Creme de Menthe (white)
Shake well with cracked ice and strain into 3 oz. cocktail glass.

VODKATINI

Same as VODKA MARTINI.

W

WALLICK COCKTAIL

1¼ oz. Dry Vermouth
1¼ oz. Old Mr. Boston Dry Gin
1 Teaspoon Curacao
*Stir well with cracked ice and strain
into 3 oz. cocktail glass.*

WARD EIGHT

Juice ½ Lemon
1 Teaspoon Powdered Sugar
1 Teaspoon Grenadine
2 oz. Old Mr. Boston Whiskey*
*Shake well with cracked ice and
strain into 8 oz. stem glass previously
prepared with 2 cubes of ice, slice of
orange, lemon and a cherry. Serve
with straws.*

WASHINGTON COCKTAIL

1½ oz. Dry Vermouth
¾ oz. Old Mr. Boston Five Star
Brandy
2 Dashes Bitters
½ Teaspoon Simple Syrup
*Stir well with cracked ice and strain
into 3 oz. cocktail glass.*

WATERBURY COCKTAIL

½ Teaspoon Powdered Sugar
Juice of ¼ Lemon or ½ Lime
White of 1 Egg
1½ oz. Old Mr. Boston Five Star
Brandy
½ Teaspoon Grenadine
*Shake well with cracked ice and
strain into 4 oz. cocktail glass.*

WEBSTER COCKTAIL

Juice ½ Lime
¼ oz. Old Mr. Boston Apricot Flavored Brandy
½ oz. Dry Vermouth
1 oz. Old Mr. Boston Dry Gin
*Shake well with cracked ice and
strain into 3 oz. cocktail glass.*

WEDDING BELLE COCKTAIL

¼ oz. Orange Juice
¼ oz. Old Mr. Boston Wild Cherry
Flavored Brandy
¾ oz. Old Mr. Boston Dry Gin
¾ oz. Dubonnet
*Shake well with cracked ice and
strain into 3 oz. cocktail glass.*

* *Bourbon, Blended, Rye or Canadian.*

WEEP NO MORE COCKTAIL

Juice ½ Lime
¾ oz. Dubonnet
¾ oz. Old Mr. Boston Five Star
Brandy
¼ Teaspoon Maraschino
Shake well with cracked ice and strain into 3 oz. cocktail glass.

WEMBLEY COCKTAIL

¾ oz. Dry Vermouth
1½ oz. Old Mr. Boston Dry Gin
¼ Teaspoon Old Mr. Boston
Apricot Flavored Brandy
½ Teaspoon Apple Brandy
Stir well with cracked ice and strain into 3 oz. cocktail glass.

WEST INDIES FROSTED COCKTAIL

See FROZEN DAIQUIRI COCKTAIL *on page 39.*

WESTERN ROSE COCKTAIL

½ oz. Old Mr. Boston Apricot Flavored Brandy
1 oz. Old Mr. Boston Dry Gin
½ oz. Dry Vermouth
¼ Teaspoon Lemon Juice
Shake well with cracked ice and strain into 3 oz. cocktail glass.

WHIP COCKTAIL

½ oz. Dry Vermouth
½ oz. Sweet Vermouth
1¼ oz. Old Mr. Boston Five Star
Brandy
¼ Teaspoon Absinthe Substitute
1 Teaspoon Curacao
Stir well with cracked ice and strain into 3 oz. cocktail glass.

WHISKEY COBBLER

Dissolve, in 10 oz. goblet,
1 Teaspoon Powdered Sugar
2 oz. Carbonated Water
Fill goblet with shaved ice; add:
2 oz. Old Mr. Boston Whiskey*
Stir well and decorate with fruits in season. Serve with straws.

WHISKEY COCKTAIL

1 Dash Bitters
1 Teaspoon Simple Syrup
2 oz. Old Mr. Boston Whiskey*
Stir well with cracked ice and strain into 3 oz. cocktail glass. Serve with a cherry.

WHISKEY COLLINS

Juice of ½ Lemon
1 Teaspoon Powdered Sugar
2 oz. Old Mr. Boston Whiskey*
Shake well with cracked ice and strain into 12 oz. Tom Collins glass. Add several cubes of ice, fill with carbonated water and stir. Decorate with slice of lemon, orange and a cherry. Serve with straws.

WHISKEY DAISY

Juice of ½ Lemon
½ Teaspoon Powdered Sugar
1 Teaspoon Raspberry Syrup or
Grenadine
2 oz. Old Mr. Boston Whiskey*
Shake well with cracked ice and strain into stein or 8 oz. metal cup. Add cube of ice and decorate with fruit.

* *Bourbon, Blended, Rye or Canadian.*

WHISKEY EGGNOG

Egg
Teaspoon Powdered Sugar
oz. Old Mr. Boston Whiskey*
ill glass with Milk. Shake well with
racked ice and strain into 12 oz.
om Collins glass. Grate nutmeg on
p.

WHISKEY FIX

uice of ½ Lemon
Teaspoon Powdered Sugar
Teaspoon Water and stir
ill glass with Shaved Ice
½ oz. Old Mr. Boston Whiskey*
se 8 oz. highball glass. Stir well.
dd slice of lemon. Serve with
raws.

WHISKEY FLIP

Egg
Teaspoon Powdered Sugar
½ oz. Old Mr. Boston Whiskey*
Teaspoons Sweet Cream (if desired)
hake well with cracked ice and
rain into 5 oz. flip glass. Grate a
ttle nutmeg on top.

WHISKEY HIGHBALL

Cube of Ice
oz. Old Mr. Boston Whiskey*
ll 8 oz. highball glass with ginger
e or carbonated water. Add twist
lemon peel, if desired, and stir.

ourbon, Blended, Rye or Canadian.

Old Mr. Boston Eggnog 30 Proof ▶

Whiskey Milk Punch

1 Teaspoon Powdered Sugar
2 oz. Old Mr. Boston Whiskey*
½ pt. Milk
Shake well with cracked ice, strain into 12 oz. Tom Collins glass and grate nutmeg on top.

Whiskey Orange

Juice of ½ Orange
1 Teaspoon Powdered Sugar
½ Teaspoon Absinthe Substitute
1½ oz. Old Mr. Boston Whiskey*
Shake well with cracked ice and strain into 8 oz. highball glass. Decorate with slice of orange and lemon.

Whiskey Rickey

1 Cube of Ice
Juice of ½ Lime
1½ oz. Old Mr. Boston Whiskey*
Fill 8 oz. highball glass with carbonated water and stir. Leave lime in glass.

Whiskey Sangaree

Dissolve ½ teaspoon powdered sugar in 1 teaspoon of water. Add:
2 oz. Old Mr. Boston Whiskey*
2 cubes of Ice.
Serve in 8 oz. highball glass. Fill balance with soda water. Stir, leaving enough room on which to float a tablespoon of Port Wine. Sprinkle lightly with nutmeg.

Whiskey Skin

Put lump of sugar into hot whiskey glass and fill two-thirds with boiling water. Add 2 oz. Old Mr. Boston Whiskey. Stir, then add twist of lemon peel and drop in glass.*

Whiskey Sling

Dissolve 1 teaspoon powdered sugar in teaspoon of water and juice ½ lemon
2 oz. Old Mr. Boston Whiskey*
2 Cubes of Ice
Serve in Old Fashioned cocktail glass and stir. Twist of lemon peel and drop in glass.

Whiskey Smash

Muddle 1 lump of sugar with
1 oz. Carbonated Water and
4 Sprigs of Green Mint
Add 2 oz. Old Mr. Boston Whiskey,* then a Cube of Ice
Stir and decorate with a slice of orange and a cherry. Twist of lemon peel. Use Old Fashioned cocktail glass.

Whiskey Sour

Juice of ½ Lemon
½ Teaspoon Powdered Sugar
2 oz. Old Mr. Boston Whiskey*
Shake well with cracked ice and strain into 6 oz. sour glass. Fill with carbonated water and stir. Decorate with a half-slice of lemon and a cherry.

Whiskey Squirt

1½ oz. Old Mr. Boston Whiskey
1 Tablespoon Powdered Sugar
1 Tablespoon Raspberry Syrup or Grenadine
Shake well with cracked ice and strain into 8 oz. highball glass and fill with carbonated water. Decorate with cubes of pineapple and straw berries.

* Bourbon, Blended, Rye or Canadian

W

WHISKEY SWIZZLE

Made same as GIN SWIZZLE (see page 43), using 2 oz. Old Mr. Boston Whiskey* instead of gin.

WHISKEY TODDY

Use Old Fashioned cocktail glass.
½ Teaspoon Powdered Sugar
2 Teaspoons Water
2 oz. Old Mr. Boston Whiskey*
1 Lump of Ice
Stir well. Twist lemon peel and drop in glass.

WHISKEY TODDY (HOT)

Put lump of sugar into hot whiskey glass and fill two-thirds with boiling water. Add 2 oz. Old Mr. Boston Whiskey.* Stir and decorate with slice of lemon. Grate nutmeg on top.

WHISPERS OF THE FROST COCKTAIL

¾ oz. Old Mr. Boston Whiskey*
¾ oz. Sherry Wine
¾ oz. Port Wine
1 Teaspoon Powdered Sugar
Shake well with cracked ice and strain into 3 oz. cocktail glass. Serve with slices of lemon and orange.

WHITE CARGO COCKTAIL

1 Small Scoop Vanilla Ice Cream
1 oz. Old Mr. Boston Dry Gin
Shake until thoroughly mixed and add water or Sauterne if the mixture is too thick. Serve in 4 oz. cocktail glass.

WHITE LADY COCKTAIL

White of 1 Egg
1 Teaspoon Powdered Sugar
1 Teaspoon Sweet Cream
1½ oz. Old Mr. Boston Dry Gin
Shake well with cracked ice and strain into 4 oz. cocktail glass.

WHITE LILY COCKTAIL

¾ oz. Triple Sec
¾ oz. Old Mr. Boston Imported Rum
¾ oz. Old Mr. Boston Dry Gin
¼ Teaspoon Old Mr. Boston Anisette
Shake well with cracked ice and strain into 3 oz. cocktail glass.

WHITE LION COCKTAIL

Juice ½ Lemon
1 Teaspoon Powdered Sugar
2 Dashes Bitters
½ Teaspoon Grenadine
1½ oz. Old Mr. Boston Imported Rum
Shake well with cracked ice and strain into 3 oz. cocktail glass.

WHITE PLUSH

Pour 2 oz. Old Mr. Boston Whiskey* into Delmonico glass. Fill balance with milk and drink without stirring.

WHITE ROSE COCKTAIL

¾ oz. Old Mr. Boston Dry Gin
½ oz. Orange Juice
Juice 1 Lime
½ oz. Maraschino
White of 1 Egg
Shake well with cracked ice and strain into 4 oz. cocktail glass.

109

Bourbon, Blended, Rye or Canadian.

WHITE WAY COCKTAIL

¾ oz. Old Mr. Boston Creme de Menthe (white)
1½ oz. Old Mr. Boston Dry Gin
Shake well with cracked ice and strain into 3 oz. cocktail glass.

WIDOW'S KISS COCKTAIL

½ oz. Yellow Chartreuse
½ oz. Benedictine
1 oz. Apple Brandy
1 Dash Bitters
Shake well with cracked ice and strain into 3 oz. cocktail glass. Strawberry may be served on top.

WIDOW'S DREAM COCKTAIL

1½ oz. Benedictine
1 Whole Egg
Shake well with cracked ice and strain into 4 oz. cocktail glass. Float 1 teaspoon of cream on top.

WINDY CORNER COCKTAIL

2 oz. Old Mr. Boston Blackberry Flavored Brandy
Stir well with cracked ice and strain into 3 oz. cocktail glass. Grate a little nutmeg on top.

XANTHIA COCKTAIL

¾ oz. Old Mr. Boston Wild Cherry Flavored Brandy
¾ oz. Yellow Chartreuse
¾ oz. Old Mr. Boston Dry Gin
Stir well with cracked ice and strain into 3 oz. cocktail glass.

X. Y. Z. COCKTAIL

½ oz. Lemon Juice
½ oz. Triple Sec
1 oz. Old Mr. Boston Imported Rum
Shake well with cracked ice and strain into 3 oz. cocktail glass.

XERES COCKTAIL

1 Dash Orange Bitters
2 oz. Sherry Wine
Stir well with cracked ice and strain into 3 oz. cocktail glass.

YALE COCKTAIL

1½ oz. Old Mr. Boston Dry Gin
½ oz. Dry Vermouth
1 Dash Bitters
1 Teaspoon Creme de Yvette
Stir well with cracked ice and strain into 3 oz. cocktail glass.

Rock and Rye 60 Proof
Peppermint Schnapps 60 Proof

Eggnog

SOME PEOPLE BELIEVE that this name is of English derivation and that "nog" comes from the word "noggin," a small drinking vessel with an upright handle. On the other hand, there are those who believe that the name is a result of joining the sounds of egg 'n grog. From whatever source, the drink itself is American dating back to about 1775. In the early days, eggnog was associated with traveling and social functions. Today it is principally associated with Easter, Thanksgiving, Christmas and New Years.

Traditionally, the liquors used in eggnog have been rum and brandy. However, whiskey, sherry, ale and cider may be used. Some of the early recipes called for milking the cow into the liquor but today, fortunately, this is unnecessary as simpler methods are now available. There are excellent nonalcoholic, prepared eggnogs to which one's favorite liquor may be added. These are available during the holiday season from virtually all dairy companies. Most of the following are simplified versions of recipes listed alphabetically in this book (for those who prefer to make their own preparations). For a complete list of recipes see the Index, page 143.

MIXING INSTRUCTIONS

A smaller or greater quantity of liquor than that called for in the following recipes may be used, depending on one's preference. Best results are obtained when all ingredients have been prechilled. Stir well, sprinkle nutmeg on top and serve in 4 oz. punch cups or glasses.

AMBASSADOR'S MORNING LIFT

qt. Prepared Dairy Eggnog
oz. Cognac
oz. Jamaica Rum
oz. Old Mr. Boston Creme de
  Cacao

ld Mr. Boston Five Star Brandy
Old Mr. Boston Bourbon Whis-
y *may be substituted for Cognac.*

BALTIMORE EGGNOG

qt. Prepared Dairy Eggnog
oz. Old Mr. Boston Five Star
  Brandy
z. Jamaica Rum
z. Madeira Wine

BRANDY EGGNOG

t. Prepared Dairy Eggnog
oz. Old Mr. Boston Five Star
  Brandy

BREAKFAST EGGNOG

t. Prepared Dairy Eggnog
oz. Old Mr. Boston Apricot Flavored Brandy
oz. Curacao

CHRISTMAS YULE EGGNOG

t. Prepared Dairy Eggnog
oz. Old Mr. Boston Whiskey*
oz. Old Mr. Boston Imported
  Rum

NERAL HARRISON'S EGGNOG

t. Prepared Dairy Eggnog
oz. Sweet Cider

IMPERIAL EGGNOG

1 qt. Prepared Dairy Eggnog
10 oz. Old Mr. Boston Five Star
  Brandy
2 oz. Old Mr. Boston Apricot Flavored Brandy

NASHVILLE EGGNOG

1 qt. Prepared Dairy Eggnog
6 oz. Old Mr. Boston Kentucky
  Bourbon Whiskey
3 oz. Old Mr. Boston Five Star
  Brandy
3 oz. Jamaica Rum

PORT WINE EGGNOG

1 qt. Prepared Dairy Eggnog
18 oz. Port Wine

RUM EGGNOG

1 qt. Prepared Dairy Eggnog
12 oz. Old Mr. Boston Imported
  Rum

SHERRY EGGNOG

1 qt. Prepared Dairy Eggnog
18 oz. Sherry Wine

WHISKEY EGGNOG

1 qt. Prepared Dairy Eggnog
12 oz. Old Mr. Boston Whiskey*

urbon, Blended, Rye or Canadian

The Martini

THOUGH THE MARTINI is viewed with almost reverent awe as drink of unique power, it is no more or less powerful than an other drink containing the same amount of alcohol.

The original Martini recipe called for one-half dry gin an one-half dry vermouth. This proportion began to change the early 1940s to two or three parts dry gin to one part d vermouth. Today, popular proportions for an Extra Dry Ma tini range from a 5–to–1 to an 8–to–1 ratio. The greater the pro portion of gin to vermouth, the "drier" the Martini.

ARE YOUR MARTINIS TOO STRONG?

Remember, America is nearly the only country in the wor. that drinks high-proof gin. The British, who perfected gin, an the Canadians prefer their gin at milder, smoother 80 proof.

To make Martinis that are extra dry but not extra strong, u 80 proof gin. The chart below shows how the trend to drier Ma tinis has increased the alcoholic content of this popular drin from a smooth 76.5 proof to a powerful 84 proof! Today's ve dry Martini can be returned to its original, more moderate pro only by using 80 proof gin.

Using Standard 36 Proof Dry Vermouth	With 90 Proof Dry Gin	Or 80 Proof Dry Gin (or Vod'
3—to—1 (Traditional)	76.5 Proof	69.0 Proof
5—to—1 (Dry)	81.0 Proof	72.6 Proof
8—to—1 (Extra Dry)	84.0 Proof	75.1 Proof

Chill 3-ounce cocktail glasses to the point of frost. Fill Martini pitcher with cracked (not crushed) ice. Ice should be dry and hard frozen. Measure out the exact ingredients for the number of drinks required, pouring in the dry gin first (gin should "smoke" as it settles over the cold ice), then the Dry Vermouth. Stir briskly until drink is very cold. Strain at once into frosty, stemmed cocktail glasses. For Martinis "on the rocks," use pre-chilled Old-Fashioned glasses and pour the liquor over cubes of ice. A twist of lemon peel (see page 125) adds a special character to a Martini which many prefer.

The following are the more popular Martinis.

MARTINI (Traditional 3–to–1)

1½ oz. Old Mr. Boston Dry Gin
½ oz. Dry Vermouth
Serve with an olive

DRY MARTINI (5–to–1)

⅔ oz. Old Mr. Boston Dry Gin
⅓ oz. Dry Vermouth
serve with an olive

EXTRA DRY MARTINI (7–to–1)

¾ oz. Old Mr. Boston Dry Gin
. oz. Dry Vermouth
serve with an olive

MARTINI (Sweet)

½ oz. Old Mr. Boston Dry Gin
. oz. Sweet Vermouth
rve with an olive. If a sweeter Martini is preferred, mix gin and sweet vermouth in equal parts.

VODKA MARTINI—VODKATINI

substitute Old Mr. Boston Vodka for Old Mr. Boston Dry Gin in any of these Martini recipes.

MARTINI (Medium)

1½ oz. Old Mr. Boston Dry Gin
½ oz. Dry Vermouth
½ oz. Sweet Vermouth
Serve with an olive

GIBSON

This is a Dry or Extra Dry Martini with a twist of lemon peel and served with one to three pearl onions. May also be made with Old Mr. Boston Vodka.

DILLATINI

A Martini substituting a Dilly Bean in place of the olive.

TEQUINI

A Martini made with Tequila instead of dry gin. Serve with a twist of lemon peel and an olive.

Bar Hints and Measurements

Here are some suggestions and fine points that will help you mix a perfect drink every time. Follow them carefully and your drinks will have the extra added touch of artistry that will mark you as a professional.

EQUIPMENT

Here is a sensible list of basic, serviceable items for even the most professional bar.

A jigger measure—designed with an accurate scale of half and quarter ounces
A sturdy mixing glass or shaker
A bar strainer
A teaspoon or set of measuring spoons
A glass stirring rod, or a long spoon—for mixing and stirring
A corkscrew, can and bottle opener
A paring knife—for paring and cutting fruit
A vacuum-type ice bucket with tongs
A wooden muddler—for mashing mint, herbs, fruits
A lemon-lime squeezer
A large pitcher—with a good pouring lip
A variety of glassware (See inside back cover)

For real elegance and professional convenience, cap every Old Mr. Boston fifth and quart with Old Mr. Boston's new Golden Pourer. See pages 70 and 149.

Use the following as a reference for determining approximately how many bottles you may need for various occasions. To be extra safe, but conservative, substitute quarts for fifths.

No. of People	For Cock- tails	You'll Need at Least	For Buffet or Dinner	You'll Need at Least	For an After- Dinner Party	You'll Need at Least
4	10 to 16 drinks	1 fifth	8 cocktails	1 fifth	12 to 16 drinks	1 fifth
			8 glasses wine	2 bottles		
			4 liqueurs	⅖ pint		
			8 highballs	1 fifth		
6	15 to 22 drinks	2 fifths	12 cocktails	1 fifth	18 to 26 drinks	2 fifths
			12 glasses wine	2 bottles		
			8 liqueurs	1 fifth		
			18 highballs	2 fifths		
8	18 to 24 drinks	2 fifths	16 cocktails	1 fifth	20 to 34 drinks	2 fifths
			16 glasses wine	3 bottles		
			10 liqueurs	1 fifth		
			18 highballs	2 fifths		
12	20 to 40 drinks	3 fifths	24 cocktails	2 fifths	25 to 45 drinks	3 fifths
			24 glasses wine	4 bottles		
			16 liqueurs	1 fifth		
			30 highballs	3 fifths		
20	40 to 65 drinks	4 fifths	40 cocktails	3 fifths	45 to 75 drinks	5 fifths
			40 glasses wine	7 bottles		
			25 liqueurs	2 fifths		
			50 highballs	4 fifths		

Even the most professional bartender measures the ingredients of every drink, even though experience may permit some to do this by eye and by skillful freehand pouring. However, to make a perfect drink every time, measure all ingredients. Remember, too, that many drinks can be spoiled by being too strong as well as too weak.

Some standard bar measures:

1 Dash	⅙ teaspoon (1/32 ounce)
1 Teaspoon (bar spoon)	⅛ ounce
1 Pony	1 ounce
1 Jigger (barglass)	1½ ounces
1 Wineglass	4 ounces
1 Split	6 ounces
1 Cup	8 ounces

Some other helpful measures:

1 Miniature (nip)	1, 1.6 or 2 ounces
1 Half pint (¼ quart)	8 ounces (1/16 gallon
1 Tenth (⅘ pint)	12.8 ounces (1/10 gallon
1 Pint (½ quart)	16 ounces (⅛ gallon)
1 Fifth (⅘ quart)	25.6 ounces (⅕ gallon)
1 Quart	32 ounces (¼ gallon)
1 Imperial Quart	38.4 ounces
1 Half gallon	64 ounces
1 Gallon	128 ounces

And some *average* dry wine and champagne bottle measures:

Split (¼ bottle)	6 to 6½ ounces	
"Pint" (½ bottle)	11 to 13 ounces	
"Quart" (1 bottle)	24 to 26 ounces	
Magnum (2 bottles)	52 ounces	
Jeroboam (4 bottles)	104 ounces	
Tappit-hen	128 ounces	(1 gallon)
Rehoboam (6 bottles)	156 ounces	(1.22 gallons)
Methuselah (8 bottles)	208 ounces	(1.625 gallons)
Salmanazar (12 bottles)	312 ounces	(2.44 gallons)
Balthazar (16 bottles)	416 ounces	(3.3 gallons)
Nebuchadnezzar (20 bottles)	520 ounces	(4.07 gallons)
Demijohn	627.2 ounces	(4.9 gallons)

GLASSWARE

All recipes in this book indicate the size and type of glass that is appropriate for each drink. For a complete list and illustration of recommended glassware, see the inside back cover.

Always use clean sparkling glassware. Keep one towel for drying and another for polishing. A stemmed glass should be used for cold drinks served without ice, like Martinis. When held, the heat of the hand will not warm the drink as it is being consumed.

HOW TO CHILL A GLASS

Cocktail glasses should be well chilled to keep the drinks refreshingly cold. If refrigerator space is not available for prechilling, fill each glass with cracked, shaved or crushed ice before mixing. When the drink is ready, empty the glass, shake out the melted ice and then pour the drink.

How to Frost a Glass

There are two types of "frosted" glass. For "frosted" drinks, glasses should be stored in a refrigerator or buried in shaved ice long enough to give each glass a white, frosted, ice-cold look and feel.

For a "sugar-frosted" glass, moisten the rim of a prechilled glass with a slice of lime or lemon and then dip the rim into powdered sugar.

Ice

Use plenty of ice. Whether cubed, cracked, crushed or shaved, all ice should be fresh, crystal-clear and free of any taste. Always put ice in the mixing glass, shaker or drinking glass before pouring any ingredients. The liquids are chilled as they are poured over the ice and there is no splashing.

Most highballs, Old Fashioneds and on-the-rocks drinks call for cubed ice. Use cracked or cubed ice for stirring and shaking; crushed or shaved ice for special tall drinks, frappés and other drinks to be sipped through straws.

Sugar

Always place sugar in the mixing glass before adding the liquor. Unless otherwise stated in the recipe, powdered sugar should be used with alcohol. Powdered sugar dissolves and blends quickest with alcohol at low temperatures.

Simple Syrup

Simple syrup may be substituted for powdered sugar in many drinks. Some bartenders claim it gives certain drinks a smoother, richer taste. Many prefer it because it blends instantly. You may make a simple syrup ahead of time and store it in bottles in a cool place. Dissolve one pound of granulated sugar in one half pint of warm water, gradually stirring in enough water to make one pint of syrup.

WHEN TO STIR

Drinks containing clear liquors and ingredients require stirring with ice for proper mixing. Stir drinks containing a carbonated mixer (tonic water, ginger ale, cola, etc.) *gently* to preserve the sparkle and effervescence. Remember, too little stirring fails to mix or chill the ingredients; too much stirring melts the ice and dilutes the drink.

WHEN TO SHAKE

Drinks containing fruit juices, sugar, eggs, cream or other ingredients difficult to mix, should be shaken briskly. For thorough blending of some punches, sours, other fruit and egg drinks, and where frothiness is desired, use an electric mixer or blender.

USING THE STRAINER

Strain all cocktails before serving with a wire—not silver—strainer. Use one with clips that permits the wire to rest within the rim of the mixing glass or shaker.

POURING

When mixing the same cocktail for four or more people, make the drinks in one batch. To make each drink of equal strength and taste set up the required number of glasses in a row. Pour, filling each glass only halfway. Then go back to the first glass and finish off.

How to Float Cordials

To make cordials or brandy float one on top of the other in the same glass, as in the Pousse Café, pour each ingredient slowly over a teaspoon held bottom side up over the glass. The rounded surface of the teaspoon will spread each cordial or brandy slowly and evenly over the one below without mixing. This may also be accomplished by first inserting a glass stirring rod into the glass and then slowly pouring each ingredient down the rod.

Be sure to pour all ingredients in the order given in the recipe.

How to Flame Liquor

The secret to setting liquor (brandy, rum, gin, whiskey) aflame in drink and cooking recipes is to make certain that glass, cooking vessel and liquor are all prewarmed. Start with a teaspoon or tablespoon of liquor, preheat over flame, then set afire. Pour flaming liquid carefully into remaining liquor to be set aflame.

Using Eggs

To separate the white of an egg from the yellow, break the egg by hitting the center on the edge of a glass. Separate the two halves, passing the yolk from one half-shell to the other until the white slips through to the glass below.

The egg always goes into the mixing glass or shaker before the liquor, to make certain that the egg is fresh. When shaking, use cubed or cracked ice to break up and blend the egg with the other ingredients.

Using Fruit and Fruit Juices

Whenever possible use only *fresh* fruit. Wash the outside peel before using. Fruit slices should be cut about one-quarter-inch thick and slit toward the center to fix slice on rim of glass. Keep garnishes fresh and cold.

When mixing drinks containing fruit juices, *always* pour the liquor last. Squeeze and strain fruit juices just before using to in sure freshness and good taste. Avoid artificial, concentrated substitutes.

Twist of Lemon Peel

When recipes call for a twist of lemon peel, rub a narrow strip of peel around the rim of the glass to deposit the oil on it. Then twist the peel so that the oil (usually one small drop) will drop into the drink. Then drop in the peel. The lemon oil gives added character to the cocktail which many prefer.

Using Bitters

Ordinarily, only a dash or two is necessary. This small but important ingredient can add zest to a great number of mixed drinks. Made from numerous and subtle combinations of roots, barks, berries and herbs, they are all characterized by their aromatic, bitter taste.

Here are a few of the best-known brands:

Angostura Bitters—made in Trinidad from an ancient, secret recipe.

Abbott's Aged Bitters—made in Baltimore by the same family since 1865.

Peychaud's Bitters—made in New Orleans.

Orange Bitters—made from the dried peel of bitter Seville oranges and sold by several English firms.

Vermouth

Vermouth is a white appetizer wine flavored with as many as thirty to forty different herbs, roots, berries, flowers and seeds. There are nearly as many vermouth formulas as there are brand labels.

The dry variety (French) is light gold in color and has a delightful nutty flavor. Sweet (Italian) vermouth is richer in flavor and more syrupy. Both are delicate and will lose their freshness if left too long in an opened bottle. Use with care and discretion in mixed drinks (follow the recipe) since most people now prefer "drier" cocktails.

The Liquor Dictionary

$\mathbb{M}$ UCH of the enjoyment of social drinking comes from a knowledge of the different types of alcoholic beverages available. This section was prepared to help you understand some of the ofttimes subtle, differences between one type of liquor and another.

First, here are a few common terms frequently misunderstood.

ALCOHOL (C_2H_5OH) the common ingredient of all liquor. There are many types of alcohol, but for beverages only ethyl alcohol is used. Of the several types of ethyl alcohol, those spirits distilled from grain, grape, fruit and cane are the most common.

PROOF–a measurement of alcoholic strength or content. One degree of proof equals one-half of 1 per cent of alcohol. An 80 proof product contains 40 per cent alcohol; a 90 proof product, 45 per cent alcohol, etc.

For centuries Scotch, British Gin and Canadian Whisky sold in England, Scotland, Canada and most of the rest of the world has been sold at mild 80 proof. America has only begun to appreciate the tasteful qualities of the more moderate lower proofs.

In recent years, a trend has developed in this country toward 80 proof blended and straight whiskeys, dry gin, Scotch and Canadian whiskies. Practically all of the *Rum* sold in America is now 80 proof. *Vodka* at 80 proof outsells the higher proof 9-to-1. For years the most expensive, famous-name Cognacs have been imported at 80 proof, and now nearly all American-made *Brandy* is 80 proof.

AGE—often believed to be the *only* indication of quality; a whiskey, rum, or brandy can be aged too long as well as not long enough. Other factors affecting quality include variables in the distilling process itself, the types of grain used, the warehousing techniques employed, the rate of aging and the degree of skill used in determining product maturity. Aging may make good whiskey better, but no amount of aging can make good whiskey out of bad.

GRAIN NEUTRAL SPIRITS—a practically tasteless, colorless alcohol distilled from grain (like whiskey) but at 190 proof or above, whereas whiskey must be distilled at less than 190 proof. Used in blended whiskeys, in making gin and vodka, and in many other liquors.

WINE—produced principally from the fermented juice of grapes. If any other fruit is used, the name of the fruit must appear on the label. The alcoholic content of wine ranges from less than 14 per cent to 21 per cent.

BEER—the name for five types of fermented malt beverages: *Lager Beer* (about 3.6 per cent alcohol), the most popular type of light, dry beer; *Ale,* having a more pronounced flavor and aroma of hops, is heavier and more bitter than lager beer; *Bock Beer, Porter* and *Stout* (about 6 per cent alcohol), which are progressively heavier, darker, richer and sweeter than either lager beer or ale.

Brandy

Brandy is distilled from a fermented mash of grapes or other fruit. These brandies, aged in oak casks, are usually bottled at either 80 or 84 proof. Long enjoyed as an after-dinner drink, brandy is also widely used in cooking.

Cognac—this fine brandy, known for its smoothness and heady dry aroma, is produced only in the Cognac region of France. (All Cognac is brandy, but not all brandy is Cognac, nor is all French brandy Cognac.)

Armagnac—is much like Cognac but has a drier taste. It is produced only in the Armagnac region of France.

American Brandy—all of which is distilled in California, has its own excellent characteristics of taste. Unlike European brandies (whose farmer-distillers sell their brandies to blender-shippers who control the brand names), California brandies are usually produced by individual firms that grow the grapes, distill, age, blend, bottle and market the brandies under their own brand names.

Apple Brandy, Apple Jack or Calvados—is distilled from a cider made from apples. Calvados is produced only in Normandy, France. Apple Jack may be bottled-in-bond under the same regulations that apply to whiskey.

Fruit-flavored Brandies—are brandy-based liqueurs produced from Blackberries, Peaches, Apricots, Cherries and Ginger. They are usually bottled at 70 or 80 proof.

Cordials

THE words Cordial and Liqueur are synonymous, describing liquors made by mixing or redistilling neutral spirits with fruits, flowers, herbs, seeds, roots, plants or juices to which sweetening has been added. Practically all cordials are sweet and colorful, with highly concentrated, dessertlike flavor.

Cordials are made in all countries. Several, made from closely guarded secret recipes and processes, are known throughout the world by their trade or proprietary brand names.

Here are brief descriptions of the cordials and flavorings mentioned most frequently in the recipes in this book:

ABSINTHE—anise seed (licorice) flavor; contains wormwood; illegal in the United States

ABSINTHE SUBSTITUTES—Abisante, Abson, Anisette, Herbsaint, Mistra, Ojen, Oxygene, Pernod

AMER PICON—bitter, orange-flavored French cordial made from quinine and spices

ANISETTE—anise seed, licorice flavor

BENEDICTINE—secret herb formula first produced by Benedictine monks

BITTERS—(see page 125)

CHARTREUSE—yellow and green herb liqueurs developed by Carthusian monks

CREME(S)—so-called because high sugar content results in cream-like consistency

    CREME DE CACAO—from cacao and vanilla beans

    CREME DE CASSIS—from black currants

    CREME DE MENTHE—from mint

    CREME DE YVETTE—from violets

CURACAO—orange-flavored, made of dried orange peel, from Dutch West Indies

DUBONNET—French aperitif wine made from aromatics, has slight quinine taste

GRENADINE—made from pomegranates, used for flavoring

KUMMEL—caraway and anise seeds and other herb flavors

MARASCHINO—liqueur made from cherries grown in Dalmatia, Yugoslavia

PASSION FRUIT (PASSIONOLA)—a nonalcoholic mix made from the Passion Flower

PEPPERMINT SCHNAPPS—a light-bodied creme de menthe

PERNOD—a French anise-flavored liqueur and absinthe substitute

ROCK AND RYE—fruit juice, rock candy and rye whiskey, bottled with fruit slices

SLOE GIN—a liqueur made from sloe berries (blackthorn bush)

SWEDISH PUNCH—Scandinavian liqueur made from Batavia Arak rum, tea, lemon and other spices. Also known as Arrack Punsch and Caloric Punsch (the latter because it gives off heat)

TEQUILA—an aged, colorless Mexican liquor of high proof made from the mescal plant. Not to be confused with Pulque, made from the same plant, but not aged and with a heavy sour milk flavor.

TRIPLE SEC—colorless Curacao, but less sweet.

Gin

GIN, which is distilled from grain, receives its flavor and aroma from juniper berries and other botanicals. (Every gin producer has his own special recipe.)

Most gin is colorless, though some brands may be golden or straw-yellow because of aging in barrels. Even though a distiller ages his gin, he cannot, by law, make age claims for his product. Gin sold around the world at 80 proof is bottled in this country at proofs varying from 80 to 94.

DRY GIN—merely signifies that the gin lacks sweetness.

VACUUM-DISTILLED DRY GIN—is distilled in a glass-lined vacuum still at a low 90° Fahrenheit temperature (instead of at the usual 212°), capturing only the light, volatile flavors and aromas without the bitterness found in some gins.

LONDON DRY GIN—originated in England and is now considered a generic term and may appear on American-made gins as well. Dry gins from England are inclined to be a little heavier-bodied.

GOLDEN GIN—is a dry gin which, due to aging in wood, has acquired a golden color.

HOLLAND, GENEVA OR SCHIEDAM GINS—are imported from Holland, where gin originated, are highly flavored and rich in aromatic oils; they do not mix well with other ingredients in cocktails.

OLD TOM GIN—is an English gin that has been sweetened with sugar syrup.

FLAVORED GIN—is a sweet gin usually flavored with orange, lemon or mint.

SLOE GIN—is not a gin at all but a liqueur. (See page 130.)

Rum

R∪M is distilled from the fermented juice of sugar cane, cane syrup and molasses at less than 190 proof (160 proof for New England rum) and bottled at not less than 80 proof. It is aged in uncharred barrels where it picks up very little coloring; dark rums often have caramel added to them for color .

Most rums are blends of several aged rums, ranging from heavy, pungent types to light, brandylike varieties, selected for special aroma, flavor and color. There are two main types of rum.

LIGHT-BODIED RUMS—are dry with only a very slight molasses flavor. Available in two varieties, White and Gold Label (or Light and Dark), the Gold or Dark is usually a bit sweeter with a more pronounced taste. Among these rums are included rums from Puerto Rico, Cuba and the Virgin Islands. Light-bodied rums are also produced in the Dominican Republic, Haiti, Venezuela, Mexico, Hawaii and the Philippines.

HEAVY-BODIED RUMS—are darker, sweeter and have a pungent bouquet, body and flavor. These are distilled by a different and slower fermentation process, which allows more time for a fuller, richer molasseslike body to develop and include rums from Jamaica, Demerara (British Guiana), Martinique, Trinidad, Barbados and New England.

Vodka

VODKA, most versatile of all alcoholic beverages, is a highly refined and filtered liquor distilled from any material at or above 190 proof, bottled at not less than 80 or more than 110 proof. It was originally made in Russia, from potatoes; but in the United States, vodka is usually distilled from grain, primarily corn and wheat. The subtle differences between various vodkas results from the types of grain used and the distilling and filtering processes employed. Most American vodkas are filtered through activated charcoal.

Vodka is not aged; it is colorless and virtually tasteless and odorless. In Russia and the Baltic countries, vodka is always taken straight and ice-cold from small glasses, at one swallow, along with food. In America, vodka is usually mixed with fruit juices, carbonated beverages and other ingredients where vodka's softness and palatability does not interfere with the taste of the main ingredient.

FLAVORED VODKA—an American-originated product. Excellent straight or in mixed drinks, it has been sweetened and flavored, usually with orange, lemon, lime, mint or grape. It is usually bottled at 70 proof.

ZUBROVKA—vodka in which a bit of special "buffalo" grass is steeped. This European grass gives the vodka a light yellowish color and a slight aromatic bouquet. It can be made at home by buying "buffalo" grass from an herb company and steeping it in vodka. Zubrovka is used like Vodka.

Whiskey

Whiskeys are distilled from a fermented mash of grain (usually corn, rye, barley or wheat), and then aged in oak barrel. In this country, whiskey must be distilled at less than 190 proof (although whiskey with a specific designation such as Bourbon, Rye, etc., cannot be distilled above 160 proof) and must be bottled at no less than 80 proof.

Whiskey, when placed in barrels to age, is a water-colored liquid. It is during the aging period that whiskey obtains it characteristic amber color, flavor and aroma.

The major whiskey-producing countries are the United States, Canada, Scotland and Ireland. Special grain characteristics, recipes and distillation processes make the whiskey of each country distinct from that of the others.

American Whiskey—Although American whiskeys fall into two major categories, straight whiskey and blended whiskey, the United States Government acknowledges thirty-three distinct types of whiskey. Only the major types (98 per cent of the nation's consumption) are covered here.

Straight Whiskey is distilled from corn, rye, barley or wheat (not blended with neutral grain spirits or any other whiskey) and aged in charred oak barrels for a minimum of two years. There are four major types of straight whiskey:

1. *Bourbon Whiskey* is distilled from a mash of grain containing not less than 51 per cent corn and is normally aged four years in new charred oak barrels. Bourbon is amber in color and full-bodied in flavor. When distilled in Kentucky it is usually referred to as *Kentucky Straight Bourbon Whiskey*. Bourbon is named for Bourbon County in Kentucky where this type of whiskey originated. Bourbon is also produced in Illinois, Indiana, Ohio, Pennsylvania, Tennessee and Missouri.

2. *Rye Whiskey* is distilled from a mash of grain containing not less than 51 per cent rye and is much like bourbon in color, but it is different in taste and heavier in flavor.

3. *Corn Whiskey* is distilled from a mash of grain containing not less than 80 per cent corn. Corn whiskey is commonly aged in re-used charred oak barrels.

4. *Bottled-in-Bond Whiskey* is straight whiskey, usually bourbon or rye, which is produced under United States Government supervision. Though the government does not guarantee the quality of bonded whiskey, it does require that the whiskey be at least four years old, that it be bottled at 100 proof, that it be produced in one distilling by the same distiller, and that it be stored and bottled at a bonded warehouse under government supervision.

Blended Whiskey—A blend of one or more straight whiskeys and neutral grain spirits containing at least 20 per cent or more straight whiskey bottled at not less than 80 proof.

1. *Kentucky Whiskey—A Blend* is a blended whiskey in which all the straight whiskeys are distilled in Kentucky.

2. *A Blend of Straight Whiskeys* occurs when two or more straight whiskeys are blended together, to the exclusion of neutral grain spirits.

CANADIAN WHISKY—Canadian whiskies are blended whiskies, usually distilled from rye, corn and barley. Produced only in Canada, under government supervision, most of the Canadian whisky sold in this country is at least four years old. Canadian whisky, usually lighter bodied than American whiskey, is sold in Canada, and in most of the world, except the United States, at 80 proof.

SCOTCH WHISKY—Produced only in Scotland, Scotch whiskies are blended whiskies deriving their individual personalities from native barley grain and traditional pot stills. All Scotch blends contain malt whisky and grain whisky (similar to American grain neutral spirits). Scotch's distinctive smoky flavor comes from drying malted barley over peat fires. All the Scotch imported into this country is at least four years old and is usually 80 or 86 proof. Scotch sold in the rest of the world is almost always 80 proof.

IRISH WHISKEY—Produced only in Ireland, Irish whiskey, like Scotch, is a blended whiskey containing both barley malt whiskeys and grain whiskeys. Unlike Scotch, however, the malt is dried in coal-fired kilns and the aroma of the fires does not reach the malt. Irish whiskey is heavier and more full-bodied than Scotch and is usually 86 proof.

Index

If you know the name of the mixed drink you desire, you need not use this index, as all drinks are listed alphabetically throughout the book.

This index is arranged so that you may choose specific types of drinks such as cocktails, fizzes, highballs, etc., or cocktails made with Vodka, Gin, Whiskey, Sloe Gin and other ingredients.

COBBLERS

These tall drinks are gener-
ally served in a large goblet.
They are made with lots of
shaved ice, fruit and liquor,
decorated with berries, fresh
fruit and, if desired, a sprig
of mint. Serve with straws.

COLLINS

These are tall, cool drinks be-
longing to the Punch family,
with Tom and John the best
known members. Any basic
liquor can be used, with the
juice of lemon or lime, over
ice cubes in a frosted, 12 oz.
highball glass, with sugar
added to taste and filled with
soda water. Garnish with a
slice of lemon and a cherry.

Fixes

These sweet "miniature" Cobblers are made in highball glasses with liquor, lemon juice, sugar and lots of shaved ice. Serve with fruits, berries and straws.

Fizzes

An early morning, midafternoon or evening pleasure, these are made from liquor, citrus juices and sugar, shaken with ice and strained into small highball glasses, which are then filled with "fizz" (soda) water, though different carbonated beverages, even Champagne, may be used. A few call for egg whites or yolks.

Eggnogs

This is a most agreeable, enriching way of taking whole eggs and milk. They can be served in cups, from a bowl, in the holiday season or in a tall, individually prepared glass. In either case, a sprinkling of nutmeg is a must.

Flips

This combination Eggnog and Fizz is made with liquor, egg and sugar, shaken well with cracked ice and strained into short-stemmed flip glasses. Good early-morning or bedtime drinks, sprinkled with nutmeg.

145

RYE WHISKEY DRINKS

(See Whiskey Drinks, on page 147 of Index)

SANGAREES

These are taller, sweet Old Fashioneds (without bitters); they may be made with whiskey, gin, rum or brandy, with port wine floated on top, or with wine, ale, porter or stout, with a sprinkle of nutmeg.

SCOTCH WHISKY DRINKS

SLINGS

These are like Sangarees, but made with the addition of lemon juice and a twist of lemon peel. Usually served in an Old Fashioned glass.

SLOE GIN DRINKS

SMASHES

These are junior-sized Juleps served in Old Fashioned glasses. Make with muddled sugar, ice cubes and whiskey, gin, rum or brandy as well; sprigs of mint and a squirt of soda water, if desired, and garnish with fruit.

SOURS

Made with lemon juice, sugar and any of the base liquors, these are tart lemon cocktails similar to a highly concentrated Punch. Decorate with a lemon slice and cherry.

SWEDISH PUNCH DRINKS

PRODUCT ILLUSTRATIONS

DECORATE WITH LABELS

In response to many requests, Old Mr. Boston now offers a variety of colorful liquor labels for use in decorating waste baskets, lamp shades, screens, room dividers, trays, table tops, home bars and other such articles. All labels are genuine, have been printed in many colors, some on gold and silver foil paper. Many are embossed and several are die-cut into attractive, interesting shapes.

For a package of 30 different labels, in a variety of sizes, complete with illustrated instructions, send $1.00 to Decorating Labels, Old Mr. Boston, Boston 18, Mass.

PEARL-WHITE POURER

Illustrated on page 46. Safe, practical and washable, they screw on, have no corks to crumble, stick or replace. Interchangeable on all Old Mr. Boston fifths and quarts. 25¢ each from Pourer, Old Mr. Boston, Boston 8, Mass.

Port

Beer Goblet

Pony

Delmonico   Sherry   Whiskey Sour   Whiskey   Highball   Old Fashioned

Saucer Champagne   Cocktail   Cordial   Fizz   Stem   Rhine Wine   Brandy Inhe